Reading First in the Classroom

Diane Barone
University of Nevada, Reno

Darrin Hardman
Nevada State Department of Education

Joan Taylor
Washoe County School District

PEARSON

Boston • New York • San Francisco
Mexico City • Montreal • Toronto • London • Madrid • Munich • Paris
Hong Kong • Singapore • Tokyo • Cape Town • Sydney

Series Editor: *Aurora Martínez Ramos*
Series Editorial Assistant: *Kevin Shannon*
Marketing Manager: *Jen Armstrong*
Production Editor: *Won Jang*
Editorial-Production Service: *Omegatype Typography, Inc.*
Manufacturing Buyer: *Andrew Turso*
Composition and Prepress Buyer: *Linda Cox*
Cover Administrator: *Rebecca Krzyzaniak*
Electronic Composition: *Omegatype Typography, Inc.*

For related titles and support materials, visit our online catalog at www.ablongman.com.

To obtain permission(s) to use material from this work, please submit a written request to Allyn and Bacon, Permissions Department, 75 Arlington Street, Boston, MA 02116, or fax your request to 617-848-7320.

Between the time Website information is gathered and then published, it is not unusual for some sites to have closed. Also, the transcription of URLs can result in typographical errors. The publisher would appreciate notification where these errors occur so that they may be corrected in subsequent editions.

Library of Congress Cataloging-in-Publication Data

CIP data not available at the time of publication.
ISBN 0-205-45454-2

Printed in the United States of America
10   9   8   7   6   5   4   3   2   1   09   08   07   06   05   04

contents

chapter five

The Implications and Issues Surrounding Reading First Legislation   87

preface

Reading First in the Classroom provides a comprehensive exploration of Reading First legislation. We believe that this book is important to teachers and educational personnel because it documents all of the critical aspects of this legislation. These aspects include a rich description of Reading First and its implications; a review of what scientifically based research is, how to find it, and how to evaluate it; all of the components of reading instruction with thorough research grounding; comprehensive descriptions of the assessments required for reading instruction and a full explanation of the critical aspects related to assessment; and discussion of the implications and issues surrounding reading instruction. The book is enriched with historical perspectives to ground the current No Child Left Behind legislation and Reading First. Perhaps most important to teachers, a detailed overview of each literacy component is presented along with its scientifically based research support and connections to practice.

Three of us have joined together to write this book. We have all spent much of our careers as classroom teachers and each of us has unique understandings and experiences that contribute to the strength and thoroughness of this book. Diane Barone began her career as a primary-grade teacher and is currently a professor of literacy at the University of Nevada, Reno. Her research has always focused on young children's literacy development, particularly in high-poverty schools. She is the principal investigator for the Reading First grant in Nevada. Darrin Hardman currently works for the Nevada Department of Education where he serves as co-director of the Nevada Reading Excellence and Reading First grants. He is also pursuing a doctoral degree in literacy at the University of Nevada, Las Vegas. In addition, he teaches undergraduate literacy courses at UNLV. Previously he taught first, second, and third grades, was a site-based literacy specialist, and worked in the Curriculum and Professional Development Department for Clark County School District. Joan Taylor is a long-time teacher in Washoe County School District and an instructor of literacy classes at University of Nevada, Reno. During a leave of absence from her school district, she served as Assistant Director of Assessments, Program Accountability, and Curriculum at the Nevada Department of Education and authored Nevada's Reading First and Nevada Reading Excellence Act grants. She has been the director of the Northern Nevada Writing Project and the Nevada State Network Writing Project, both sites of the National Writing Project. She is currently completing her doctoral dissertation on elementary writing instruction in a historical context.

We have organized the chapters in the book to move from the foundational information about Reading First to the details surrounding Reading First legislation. Chapter 1 opens with the background of Reading First, including its reliance on the results of the National Reading Panel (NRP) report. It provides key information about the expectations of this grant, such as scientifically based reading programs, assessments, professional development, and partnerships and collaboration. It ends with practical suggestions for teachers working with state Reading First efforts.

Chapter 2 builds from this foundation and addresses what scientifically based reading research is and how it affects day-to-day instruction in classrooms. In this chapter there is an overview of research designs and the contributions each makes to understanding student learning and instruction. The next portion of this chapter provides information on finding quality research and on critically reading it. The chapter ends by providing teachers with locations to find research that they can transform into exemplary classroom practice.

Chapter 3 is the heart of the book. This chapter focuses on each essential component of reading instruction as identified by the National Reading Panel. Each element is carefully described and its research base is presented. Once the research base has been established, the element's place in classroom instruction is described. Each section ends with a checklist to help teachers assess their use of the element in their own classrooms. Issues such as round-robin reading and decodable text are also discussed.

Chapter 4 shifts focus to assessments. This chapter provides the historical background of assessment and transitions to the assessment that is expected as part of Reading First legislation. After the discussion on screening, diagnosis, progress monitoring, and outcome-based assessment, the scientific basis for assessments is explored. Teachers can understand assessment issues that center on reliability and validity. The chapter closes with assessment targeted to each essential component of reading.

The final chapter of the book, Chapter 5, considers the implications centered on Reading First. This chapter begins with an exploration of the historical background of other legislation, reports, and books and how they have influenced classroom instruction. It then moves from this broader context to one more focused on Reading First and its potential negative and positive implications.

Clearly, the focus of this book is Reading First and its implications for classroom teachers. We know that the expectations of this legislation cannot be achieved without thoughtful, knowledgeable teachers. We recognize that it is the teacher who makes the difference in the learning experiences of students as he or she implements research-based practices to meet the learning needs and strengths of individual students. Throughout our teaching careers we have observed excellent teacher colleagues who share and support one another, especially in times of such directives. Therefore, from our perspectives as teachers and teacher educators, we would like to share not only what Reading First is mandated to be, but also what teachers can make it become as they put reading as well as each individual student first. It is our hope that this book will serve teachers well as they strive to have all children become successful readers and writers.

Acknowledgments

We would like to thank the following reviewers for their comments on the manuscript: Judy Mazur, Buena Vista Elementary; Debra Price, Sam Houston State University; and Mary-Kate Sableski, University of Dayton.

chapter one

What Is Reading First?

Ellen is a third-grade teacher in an inner-city U.S. school where she has been teaching for eighteen years. The first thing you notice about her is her eyes—they smile. Her clear brown eyes sparkle with intelligence and good humor, even on the bad days. She has never regretted choosing teaching as a career, although some days have proven to be more wearing than rewarding. Ellen teaches because she loves being with children and watching them learn and grow.

On a drizzly spring morning, Ellen has joined the rest of the faculty in the cramped school library for a meeting to hear the news: Their school has been selected as a Reading First school for next year. She quietly finishes her coffee as Sarah belatedly

slips into the stackable blue library chair beside her. This is Sarah's first year of teaching and she is in the first-grade classroom across the hall from Ellen's. She is young, enthusiastic, energetic, and eager to become a successful teacher. She turns to Ellen as she hears the news and asks, "What is Reading First?"

In this era of Jeopardy-like question responses, the answer "Reading First" elicits such quips as, "What should you be doing prior to taking any new medicine?" or "What is the reason math comes second?" Retorts such as these are sometimes reactionary, a way of dealing with authoritative changes from new attendance procedures (just when you were finally able to master the last one) to switching grade levels (not too much difference between first graders and sixth graders except one group is a little taller, right?). Well-intentioned reform strategies are long-standing and routine for teachers, as are the unintended consequences of their efforts. Therefore, understanding the Reading First legislation, its implications and components, as well as its intended benefits, can be the first step in being informed so you and your colleagues can make it work for your students and your school.

Background

Reading First is a federal program established as a part of the No Child Left Behind (NCLB) Act of 2001 that President George W. Bush signed into law in January 2002. NCLB is a reauthorization of the Elementary and Secondary Education Act of 1965 and consists of an introduction followed by Titles I through IX. Reading First is in Title I, "Improving the Academic Achievement of the Disadvantaged," subpart B, "Student Reading Skills Improvement Grants." Its primary goal is to ensure that all children in U.S. schools will learn to read well by the end of third grade. A bipartisan majority of Congress authorized over $900 million per year for all states based on a state funding formula to provide resources to improve reading instruction. Both major political parties and both congressional houses saw this as an opportunity to support educators in their work with students in the earliest stages of literacy development.

How may this have impacted your state? Beginning in 2002, many states began applying for Reading First funds to establish research-based reading programs for students in kindergarten through third grade and to prepare classroom teachers to effectively screen, diagnose, and make instructional decisions using classroom-based reading assessments. In addition, state grants were designed to provide for increased professional development to ensure that all K–3 teachers and all special education teachers would have the skills needed to teach reading effectively. The overall granting period for states is designated for six years; a progress check at year three, in which states and districts receiving grants are required to show K–3 reading progress, is necessary for continued Reading First funding.

Each Reading First state grant includes the means of providing competitive subgrants to local districts or agencies to improve reading instruction and achievement for selected K–3 classrooms and schools. In addition, if your state is a Reading First state, it has ensured a provision for high-quality professional development in the key elements of reading instruction for all K–3 and all K–12 special education teachers through coordinated efforts with other federal, state, and local initiatives.

The National Reading Panel

At the request of Congress, the National Reading Panel (NRP), a group for education and health researchers, compiled a report of research-based knowledge on reading, including the effectiveness of various approaches used to teach children to read. Based on the National Research Council Committee's *Preventing Reading Difficulties in Young Children* (Snow, Burns, & Griffin, 1998), the following topics were studied:

- Alphabetics
    Phonemic awareness instruction
    Phonics instruction
- Fluency
- Comprehension
    Vocabulary instruction
    Text comprehension instruction
    Teacher preparation and comprehension strategies instruction
- Teacher education and reading instruction
- Computer technology and reading instruction (National Institute of Child Health and Human Development, 2000)

The NRP report, in its entirety and in a summarized version, was systematically disseminated to teachers, administrators, and state departments throughout the United States. These findings became the basis for state planning efforts for Reading First subgrants.

The Reading First Definition of Reading

For the purposes of the Reading First legislation, reading is defined as a complex system of deriving meaning from print that requires all of the following:

- The skills and knowledge to understand how phonemes, or speech sounds, are connected to print
- The ability to decode unfamiliar words
- The ability to read fluently

- Sufficient background information and vocabulary to foster reading comprehension
- The development of appropriate active strategies to construct meaning from print
- The development and maintenance of a motivation to read (United States Department of Education, n.d.)

Scientifically Based Reading Programs

The National Research Council (Snow, Burns, & Griffin, 1998) and the National Reading Panel (2000) have provided educators and policy makers with a compelling body of evidence about the complexities of literacy learning as well as some tangible evidence for better understanding how it can be developed, nurtured, and taught. Research holds much promise for us as practitioners in understanding and dealing with the serious gap in achievement between children from different social, racial, and linguistic backgrounds. In bringing researchers and teachers together to share knowledge and information, important advances can be made in the ability to meet the literacy needs of all children. Scientifically based research, as defined by the legislation, is research that:

- Applies rigorous, systematic, and objective procedures to obtain valid knowledge relevant to reading development, reading instruction, and reading difficulties and is grounded on a solid theoretical or research foundation
- Employs systematic empirical methods that draw on observation or experiment
- Involves rigorous data analyses that are adequate to test the stated hypotheses and justify the general conclusions drawn
- Relies on measurement or observational methods that provide valid data across evaluators and observers and across multiple measurements and observations
- Has been accepted by a peer-reviewed journal or approved by a panel of independent experts through a comparably rigorous, objective, and scientific review (U.S. Department of Education, n.d.)

Comprehensive reading programs with materials based on scientific reading research are an integral part of Reading First classrooms. When reviewing research findings to determine whether the program and materials are based on the criteria specified in the Reading First law, certain questions can guide decisions on how well the research meets each of the criteria. Examples of the types of questions that address criteria are included in Table 1.1.

The essential components of Reading First programs, based on the National Reading Panel report to Congress, contain scientifically based instruction on:

- Phonemic awareness
- Phonics
- Vocabulary development
- Reading fluency, including oral reading skills
- Reading comprehension (See more on the essential components in Chapter 3.)

TABLE 1.1 Scientifically Based Research, as Defined by Reading First Legislation

Criteria	Questions
Use of rigorous, systematic, and empirical methods	• Does the work have a solid theoretical or research foundation? • Was it carefully designed to avoid biased findings and unwarranted claims of effectiveness? • Does the research clearly delineate how the study was conducted, who conducted it, and on whom it was conducted? • Does it explain what procedures were followed to avoid spurious findings?
Adequacy of the data analyses to test the stated hypotheses and justify the general conclusions drawn	• Was the research designed to minimize alternative explanations for observed effects? • Are the observed effects consistent with the overall conclusions and claims of effectiveness? • Does the research present convincing documentation that the observed effects were the result of intervention? • Does the research clearly define the populations studied (i.e., does it describe the participants' ages, as well as their demographic, cognitive, academic, and behavioral characteristics?) Does it describe to whom the findings can be generalized? • Does the study provide a full description of the outcome measures?
Reliance on measurements or observational methods that provided valid data across evaluators and observers and across multiple measurements and observations	• Are the findings based on a single investigator–single classroom study, or were similar findings observed by multiple investigators in numerous locations? • What procedures were in place to minimize researcher biases? • Do observed results hold up over time? • Are the study interventions described in sufficient detail to allow for replicability? • Does the research explain how instructional fidelity was ensured and assessed?
Acceptance by a peer-reviewed journal or approved by a panel of independent experts through a comparably rigorous, objective, and scientific review	• Has the research been carefully reviewed by unbiased individuals who were not part of the research study? • Have the findings been subjected to external scrutiny and verification?

Source: From United States Department of Education, 2002.

A guide to the selection and adoption of research-based core reading programs was provided by the University of Oregon (Simmons & Kame'enui, n.d.) and made available to Reading First states and local education agencies. A series of guiding questions is included in *A Consumer's Guide to Evaluating a Core Reading Program Grades K–3: A Critical Elements Analysis* to provide direction for teacher leaders in making adoption decisions with a core reading program. (It is available online at www.pen.k12.va.us/VDOE/Instruction/Reading/ConsumerGuideReading.pdf.)

Comprehensive programs in Reading First schools include specific objectives with defined targets to measure achievement goals. Assessments on the essential elements inform teachers' instructional decisions and choices of materials and programs. The issues surrounding the adoption of a comprehensive reading program are challenging for novice and experienced teachers alike. Whereas some of us find the prescriptive formats of a number of them too restrictive to meet the needs of all our students, others find the structure helpful in planning and delivering instruction. Technical details of program organization and delivery can sometimes obscure the important issue of purposeful reading and writing as the ultimate goal of instruction. Motivation and opportunities to read and write and the availability of appropriate and varied materials to read and respond to are all essential components of comprehensive reading programs. Such programs are best directed by a site-based community of professionals. In understanding the interests and needs of individual children, classroom teachers or family members with day-to-day student contact offer engaging and purposeful content and practice in tandem with programs and materials. (See Chapter 5 for more information on the issue of scientifically based reading programs and materials.)

Assessment and Data Analysis

Reading First schools compile evaluative information on children who are experiencing reading difficulties through screening, diagnosis, and classroom-based instructional reading assessments so that early intervention and assistance can support those students' needs to become successful readers. This information supports instructional decisions for choosing appropriate interventions and materials to ensure that all students can become successful in literacy activities.

Learning to read and write is a continuous process, beginning with exposure to oral language and written language prior to formal instruction. Assessments can provide insight about early literacy acquisition with implications for instruction and early interventions. Because learning and teaching are processes that are too dynamic to rely on single measures, especially in literacy, multiple assessment measures are necessary to evaluate progress and inform instruction. Reading First schools must indicate that all available assessment measures are included in aggregating student data for instructional decisions, including state and district administered assessments.

Through the assessment process teachers will be provided with screening, diagnosis, progress monitoring, and outcome-based information on students, as seen in Table 1.2. This table highlights the purpose of each type of assessment.

Reading First legislation offered assistance to state and local educational agencies in selecting and administering assessment instruments in screening, diagnostic, and classroom-based instructional assessments. A commissioned report was provided by the University of Oregon (Kame'enui, 2002) to document the process, criteria, decision rules, guidelines, rationale, and procedures to identify screening, diagnostic, and progress monitoring reading assessments. (You can find the final report online at http://idea.uoregon.edu/assessment/.)

States must submit annual progress reports and a midpoint progress report (after three years) to show improvement in order for funding to continue. Districts and schools are responsible for documenting student achievement and growth of student populations to maintain funding.

Professional Development

Although this initiative may seem unique in its scope and efforts, it is helpful to remember that every generation of teachers has had its share of similar initiatives. During the 1830s, it was the institution of normal schools for teacher training, the abolishment of corporal punishment, and the use of extrinsic rewards and punishments for academic achievement (Katz, 1968/2001). In the late nineteenth century, curriculum policy committees attempted to mandate college preparation coursework for all students. High school teachers maintained they were in the best position to develop and provide a practical education for all students, rather than college preparation for a few. This ultimately resulted in the formation of the National Council of Teachers of English, a prominent group in curriculum reform today (National Council of Teachers of English, 1912). Every generation of educators has successfully met and dealt with reform mandates by keeping students' best interests in the forefront. There is no reason to believe that our generation of teachers will not do the same. The resiliency and adaptability of teachers, in light

TABLE 1.2   **Reading First Assessment Program**

Screening	Diagnosis	Progress Monitoring	Outcome-Based
Assessments that are administered to determine which children are at risk for reading difficulty and which will need additional intervention	Assessments that help teachers plan instruction by providing in-depth information about students' skills and instructional needs	Assessments that determine if students are making adequate progress or need more intervention to achieve grade-level reading outcomes	Assessments that provide a bottom-line evaluation of the effectiveness of the reading program

of their students' welfare, is a remarkable tribute to the successes of the U.S. education system over the past 200 years.

As part of what will surely be labeled the *standards movement* era in education histories, the International Reading Association developed standards for reading professionals in 1992 and revised them in 2003. They state that as reading professionals, we need to be knowledgeable about:

- Philosophies and theories of reading instruction
- Language development, cognition, and learning
- The reading process

In addition, they suggest the following teaching standards:

1. Have knowledge of the foundations of reading and writing processes and instruction.

2. Use a wide range of instructional practices, approaches, methods, and curriculum materials to support reading and writing instruction.

3. Use a variety of assessment tools and practices to plan and evaluate effective reading instruction.

4. Create a literate environment that fosters reading and writing by integrating foundational knowledge, use of instructional practices, approaches and methods, curriculum materials, and the appropriate use of assessments.

5. View professional development as a career-long effort and responsibility. (Professional Standards and Ethics Committee, International Reading Association, 2003)

A key goal of Reading First is to provide professional development for teachers in scientifically based reading instruction, often through the use of site- or community-based literacy leaders. Literacy leaders are teachers who exhibit leadership in subject matter knowledge, teaching experience, and the ability to work collaboratively and productively within and across school sites to develop literacy knowledge, skills, and positive dispositions of teaching colleagues. In order to enhance and support these teacher leaders, Reading First professional development includes three components:

1. Enhancing teachers' content knowledge
2. Assisting teachers in the development of strategies that can be used for continuous inquiry and improvement of teaching practice
3. Developing literacy leadership skills and dispositions

What has been clear to those of us in the teaching profession for many years is now being supported by education research that consistently and emphatically states that the single most important factor in increased student achievement is good teaching (Darling-Hammond, 1996). Numerous studies (Brophy & Good, 1986; Ferguson, 1991; Wright, Horn, & Sanders, 1997) show that investment in teacher quality, more than any other use of school resources, influences improvement in student achievement.

It is important to note that the best classroom teachers have a thorough understanding of scientifically based reading research and are masterful classroom organizers as well as skillful managers of human resources. They provide a quantity of engaging, academically rich, and connected activities for their students. Their high expectations and faith in their students' abilities are evident as they reinforce students' achievements (Pressley, 1998). Effective professional development promises to not only improve student achievement and support consistent implementation and evaluation of comprehensive reading programs, but it also may increase faculty morale, group effort, and commitment.

Collaboration of all regular classroom teachers, specialists, and administrators toward the common goals of student learning and achievement will provide sustained, organized, and comprehensive instruction for competent student outcomes and support for dedicated professionals. Objective assessment data, as well as teacher observations and perceptions, can provide the basis for professional development formats. The routine use of efficient measures of critical skills can be used to alter instruction to meet the individual class and student needs.

Pressley, Rankin, and Yokoi (2000) found in their detailed survey of well-respected primary teachers that teachers need a variety of approaches and different types of instruction to meet the infinite classroom situations they will face when teaching reading. Several researchers (Fullan, 1993; Sarason, 1996) have found that teachers react to change more productively when they have ownership of the change and they can see how it fits with their individual situations and students.

Formats of professional development should vary with the routines of the school, the needs of the staff, and the availability of resources to provide the instruction. Continuous, varied professional development may occur at many levels and in a variety of formats such as those listed below.

- Summer institutes
- Grade-level meetings
- Online synchronous or asynchronous formats
- Whole or half day in-service workshops
- Traditional courses for credit
- In-class coaching situations
- Video-assisted instruction

An ongoing format is an especially useful technique for novice teachers with follow-up sessions to assist with understanding the theory behind the practice, as well as contextualizing the practice around what comes before and after. Literacy coaches themselves need support too. Meeting with others who are working on the same tasks is helpful in supporting their work and is a means by which schools can share successful implementations and work at solving similar dilemmas. (For more information on professional development visit the National Staff Development Council website at www.nsdc.org.)

Reading First Academies

Many Reading First states are using the reading academy model to deliver professional development and to focus on their specific state standards. Most academies are designed for K–3 teachers; however, many states include K–12 special education teachers, administrators, and all teachers who provide instructional support to K–3 students and K–12 special education students. Some states have encouraged groups of teachers from a single site to attend together so they can collaborate at the academy and hold follow-up continuity sessions. These academies are generally offered for several days and include:

• *Essential elements of reading.* These are the elements defined in the National Reading Panel's report. They include phonemic awareness, systematic phonics, fluency, vocabulary, comprehension, and motivation. Most states are also including spelling and writing as integral parts of a comprehensive literacy program. This content is being delivered by highly knowledgeable and experienced reading instructors who are experts in scientifically based reading education.

• *Assessments.* Teachers in Reading First states will be provided with professional development not only in the use of instructional programs and materials, but also in the purposes and applications of assessment measures in the key components. They will receive training and practice in the administration of the assessments and the scoring procedures. Assistance will be provided in interpretation of assessment results and their implications for instruction.

Partnerships and Collaboration

All teachers, support staff, administrators, parents, and students need to be a part of the team effort in understanding and progressing toward a site's Reading First goals. Parental connections are reported in several studies analyzing effective schools (Henderson, 1987; Snow et al., 1998). Awareness of the teaching and learning practices that are occurring in classrooms on a regular basis can provide opportunities to support and supplement classroom learning with additional activities and events in other home and school situations.

Reading strategies can be shared with parents through newsletters, parent meetings, dial-a-message recordings, or websites. Books can be made available through school or local library visits, book exchanges, student reward incentives, or door prizes for attendance at family literacy events. Students need engaging books to read independently and successfully and also books that are increasingly difficult and can be read with instructional support. These events can help get these books to students.

Collaborative planning, with varying levels of participation, can be open to all interested stakeholders in a site's literacy plan. Literacy events such as reading/writing nights, published student collections, book exchanges, student presentations of oral or dramatic productions, and parent–teacher conferences are just a few ways to establish and maintain the home–school connection. We have observed that collective efforts with all stakeholders at a site provide greater impact and smoother transitions in school change and in focusing school efforts on Reading First goals.

Teaching partnerships in which a shared respect for expertise and judgments are evident among colleagues is probably one of the strongest professional development models available to Reading First classrooms. The interests and needs vary with any group of individuals and should be attended to in devising professional development efforts for site staff. Individual professional goals, both short term and long term, can be supported administratively and personally by partnerships and collaboration (Lieberman & Miller, 1998).

It is helpful to have an honest critique of a teaching lesson. This can be accomplished on an individual basis through audio or video taping teacher instruction. Reviewing and self-critiquing a lesson is often a very valuable practice. However, with the number of diverse learners in Reading First classrooms and the established fact that not all students learn in the same ways, perhaps the most valuable assistance we can provide one another is through systematic observation of the student learners. Many wonderfully taught lessons have engaged the vast majority of our students, but were unable to reach every student in a class. The reasons are varied and sometimes have no correlation to the level and manner of instruction. Outside influences, prior misconceptions on a student's part, or lack of essential background knowledge are some factors for consideration. Therefore, a colleague who is focusing on that child—who can question and analyze that student's lack of understanding—can provide a teacher with more help than one who offers constructive criticism that a teacher is able to self-determine.

How Teachers Can Work with State Reading First Efforts

The success of this initiative will depend, like most educational reforms, on the teachers who choose to provide the collaborative leadership at the classroom and site levels to make it thrive. Here are some tips for working within your own state and local Reading First initiative to ensure success for you and your students.

Listen

Actively listen to what others are saying and what the data is indicating within the context of your own site's goals and plans. Listen to your students; they will tell you what is working and not working for them, although they may not know why. Students should always be reading with the intention of making meaning. Modeling the use of self-assessment and self-correction strategies will provide them with the ability to be good listeners and will lead them on the way to independent literacy skills.

Network with Colleagues

Work to establish a school literacy team that thrives on creating possibilities and concrete plans for viable solutions. This team can be responsible for prioritizing tasks, setting timelines, and establishing how projects can be performed and what human and material resources can be gathered to accomplish a project. A core team that guides the site's shared vision can facilitate the work and also provide support during the difficult times when modification or elimination of some aspect of a plan may be necessary.

Be Wary of Quick-Fix Commercial Models

Ground the teaching of reading on sound theory dealing with how children learn and, in particular, how your specific group of students can best learn to read and write based on scientific research methods. Professional organizations such as the International Reading Association (www.reading.org) and the National Council of Teachers of English (www.ncte.org) are continuing to build large databases of curriculum materials to share with colleagues nationwide.

Turn Problems into Research Questions

By assuming the role of a researcher, teachers and learners make use of their own learning experiences as supported by existing or ongoing research on gathering and analyzing practices and progress. The inquiry perspective establishes a professional and productive stance to problems and opens the way to possible solutions and action plans rather than fostering defensive or despondent reactions. By assuming an active research-practitioner role in the developing research agenda, the work done is relevant, geared to the needs of adult and student learners, and its value is recognized by other teachers.

Speak Up—Share Your Convictions with Administrators, Parents, and the Press

You need to be your own press/public relations corps. Develop ways of expressing what you think and feel in a manner that others can hear and understand. Use "I believe" or "I have found" rather than "I think" statements when describing classroom practice based on sound theory and research. You have important stories to tell; you must tell them.

Stay Positive

Your attitude and positive energy will buoy your students and your colleagues to share in the successes and the setbacks that are sure to be a part of this hard work. Your students' feelings of success and competence as readers and writers are often dependent on your reactions to their attempts. Provide many opportunities for students to be successful in reading aloud and writing in all curricular areas. Be good to yourself. Watch for negative or self-defeating talk. Work at replacing this with positive monologues. Surround yourself with other positive individuals.

Stay Focused on Your Students

Reading First supplies the means by which teachers can systematically review and analyze assessment data and use the results to inform instruction. Close attention to students' reading strategies, the strategies used or ignored, and the types of text that seem to be difficult can provide much information to a reading teacher.

Conclusion

Using research from the National Reading Panel, Reading First is designed to ensure students' reading progress so that all children in the United States will be reading proficiently by the end of third grade. With scientifically based reading instruction, valid and reliable assessment instruments, and highly qualified teaching professionals, the United States will be in a position to meet student needs in acquiring the literacy and thinking tools necessary for active participation in a democratic and diverse society.

What is Reading First? More than anything it is a professional opportunity to provide the best possible educational experience for your students and for yourself. It is a chance to

- Identify and provide needed instructional support for the lowest performing populations of learners
- Work with the most current research and instructional practices
- Collaborate with like-minded professionals
- Be on the cutting edge of school change process
- Participate in a school community that values literacy and where children come to understand reading as an integral part of their lives

Reading First Information Websites

Reading First website: www.ed.gov/programs/readingfirst/index.html
> Provides information on Reading First state initiatives and progress.

North Central Regional Educational Laboratory website: www.ncrel.org/rf/legis.htm
> Provides information on Reading First background and legislation.

References

Brophy, J., & Good, T. (1986). Teacher behavior and student achievement. In M. Wittrock (Ed.), *Handbook of research on teaching* (pp. 328–375). New York: Macmillan.

Darling-Hammond, L. (1996). *What matters most: Teaching for America's future.* Report of the National Commission on Teaching and America's Future. Retrieved February 15, 2004, from http://www.nctaf.org/publications/WhatMattersMost.pdf.

Ferguson, R. (1991). Paying for public education: New evidence on how and why money matters. *Harvard Journal on Legislation, 28,* 465–498.

Fullan, M. (1993). *Change forces: Probing the depths of educational reform.* London: Falmer Press.

Henderson, A. T. (Ed.). (1987). *The evidence continues to grow: Parent involvement improves student achievement.* Columbia, MD: National Committee for Citizens in Education.

Kame'enui, E. J. (2002). *An analysis of reading assessment instruments for K–3.* Retrieved February 15, 2004, from http://idea.uoregon.edu/assessment/final_report.pdf.

Katz, M. B. (2001). *The irony of early school reform: Educational innovation in mid-nineteenth century Massachusetts.* Cambridge, MA: Harvard University Press. (Originally published 1968)

Lieberman, A., & Miller, L. (1999). *Teachers—Transforming their world and their work.* New York: Teachers College Press.

National Council of Teachers of English (NCTE). (1912). Proceedings of the first annual meeting, Chicago, December 1 and 2, 1911. *English Journal, 1*(1), 30–45.

National Institute of Child Health and Human Development (NICHHD). (2000). *The report of the National Reading Panel. Teaching children to read: An evidence-based assessment of the scientific research literature on reading and its implications for reading instruction* (NIH Publication No. 00-4769). Washington, DC: U.S. Government Printing Office. (Available online at www.nichd.nih.gov/publications/nrp/report.htm.)

National Reading Panel (NRP). (2000). *Teaching children to read: An evidence-based assessment of the scientific research literature on reading and its implications for reading instruction.* Washing-

ton, DC: National Institute of Child Health and Human Development.

No Child Left Behind Act (NCLB). P.L. 107-279, signed by President George W. Bush November 5, 2001, amended P.L. 107-100, pp. 1425–2093, signed by President George W. Bush January 8, 2002.

Pressley, M. (1998). *Reading instruction that works: The case for balanced teaching.* New York: Guilford.

Pressley, M., Rankin, J., & Yokoi, L. (2000). A survey of instruction practices of primary teachers nominated as effective in promoting literacy. In R. D. Robinson, M. C. McKenna, & J. M. Wedman (Eds.), *Issues and Trends in Literacy Education* (2nd ed., pp. 10–43). Boston: Allyn and Bacon.

Professional Standards and Ethics Committee, International Reading Association. (2003). *Standards for reading professionals—Revised 2003.* Newark, DE: International Reading Association. (Available online at http://www.reading.org/advocacy/standards/standards03_revised.)

Sarason, S. B. (1996). *The culture of the school and the problem of change.* New York: Teachers College Press.

Simmons, D. C., & Kame'enui, E. J. (n.d.). *A consumer's guide to evaluating a core reading program grades K–3: A critical elements analysis.* Retrieved February 15, 2004, from http://www.pen.k12.va.us/VDOE/Instruction/Reading/ConsumerGuideReading.pdf.

Snow, C. E., Burns, S., & Griffin, P. (Eds.). (1998). *Preventing reading difficulties in young children.* Washington, DC: National Academy Press. (Available as an e-book at http://www.nap.edu/html/prdyc.)

United States Department of Education. (n.d.). *Part B—Student reading skills improvement grants: Subpart 1—Reading First.* Retrieved February 15, 2004, from http://www.ed.gov/policy/elsec/leg/esea02/pg4.html.

Wright, S. P., Horn, S. P., & Sanders, W. L. (1997). Teacher and classroom context effects on student achievement: Implications for teacher evaluation. *Journal of Personnel Evaluation in Education, 11,* 57–67.

chapter two

What Is Scientifically Based Reading Research? How Does It Affect My Classroom?

Ellen is familiar with much of the latest education research. She earned her master's degree several years ago at the local university. One thing she has discovered is that research does not

remain the same over the years. One year's findings are sometimes refuted the next year or maybe even decades later. She occasionally becomes impatient with research showing methods that work for *most* children when she is concerned about helping *all* her students. She knows that the teaching and learning techniques that only work for a small fraction of students are the very ones she might need for one or two of her own. She is wondering which will become the preferred studies and methods for Reading First.

Sarah likes to hear about research findings, but she believes reading through pages of statistics and reports is a waste of her time. She would rather browse for teaching ideas to try with her first-grade students. She is hopeful that the Reading First research base will support some of the things she has heard about from teacher friends, and she is eager to try it out in her own classroom next fall. This first year she learned much more than she had imagined possible. She plans to spend a portion of her summer revising some of her lessons to ensure greater success next year.

As Ellen and Sarah depart for the summer break, they are wondering about the scientifically based reading research connected to Reading First and what it will mean for them, their students, and their school.

Does current reading research impact the instruction that teachers provide to students? In the past most of us would have responded "probably not" or "never." Most teachers would have replied that they used common sense, were eclectic, and valued their personal experience in teaching more than they did the work of educational researchers. Reading research was for others and did not affect the day-to-day experiences of teachers or children in any direct way. In addition, teachers predominantly relied on basal texts to provide support for reading instruction. They trusted core reading programs or basals with supplementary-level text to provide the key instructional strategies and text support needed to facilitate their students' reading development.

However, No Child Left Behind legislation (United States Department of Education, 2003) has changed the way teachers work. This legislation, which includes Reading First and other federal grant programs, now requires that teachers use scientifically based reading practices in their instruction. In fact, the No Child Left Behind Act of 2001 contains more than 100 references to scientifically based research and its importance to literacy instruction (McEwan & McEwan, 2003). This legislation has generated conversations and debates about what constitutes scientific inquiry and the practices associated with it (National Reading Panel, 2000; Snow, Burns, & Griffin, 1998). These debates often leave teachers frustrated as they strive to find appropriate learning experiences for the students they teach. It has even resulted in critical examination of the basals they have come to know and trust.

This chapter provides background on the various types of reading research and how they inform practice. It also presents guidelines for teachers to evaluate the research they read and the practices and materials they employ in their classrooms. The chapter ends with practical support for teachers in using research-based practices in their classrooms and in the evaluation of the core materials they use.

What Exactly Is Scientifically Based Research?

The NCLB act defined what the expectations are for research to be considered scientifically based. There are two important parts to this definition. The first stipulates that research be rigorous, systematic, and use objective procedures to obtain reliable and valid knowledge relevant to educational activities and programs. The second part of this definition further explains the following necessary characteristics of this research. Scientific research must include

1. Systematic, empirical methods that draw on observation or experiment
2. Rigorous data analyses that are adequate to test the stated hypotheses and justify the general conclusions drawn
3. Measurements or observational methods that provide reliable and valid data across evaluators and observers, across multiple measurements and observations, and across studies by the same or different investigators
4. Experimental or quasi-experimental designs in which individuals, entities, programs, or activities are assigned to different conditions and with appropriate controls to evaluate the effects of the condition of interest, with a preference for random-assignment experiments, or other designs to the extent that those designs contain within-condition or across-condition controls
5. Experimental studies that are presented clearly and in sufficient detail to allow for replication or offer the opportunity to build systematically on the findings
6. Acceptance by a peer-reviewed journal or approval by a panel of independent experts through a comparably rigorous, objective, and scientific review

For most of us this description of scientific research is distant, vague, and presented in language that is not very familiar. We hope to make this language more understandable in this chapter and others. In Chapter 4, descriptions of validity and reliability are thoroughly discussed. In this chapter, descriptions of the most frequently used research designs are provided to help teachers understand the purposes of each.

Research Designs

Quantitative Studies

Quantitative research involves the use of numerical indices to summarize, describe, and explore relationships among variables. These studies rely on control, statistics, measurements, and experiments. They can generally be grouped into studies that (1) involve experiments in which the researcher has control over variables and

(2) nonexperimental studies in which the researcher describes a phenomenon or a relationship among variables (McMillan & Wergin, 2002).

Experiments and quasi-experiments.   Experimental studies are used to answer causal questions—they seek to find cause–effect relationships. In this research design, a researcher manipulates one or more variables and observes the effect of the manipulation through an intervention. Randomized experiments are the gold standard requested by the Federal government. This makes sense because policy makers are held accountable for their decisions and they want research that provides verifiable, easily understood results (Kamil, 2004). The government also works with limited resources, which results in the need to identify strategies and materials—most often programs—that are most effective in helping children learn to read.

Most teachers are familiar with the elements of experimental research that require randomization—children, classes, or schools are randomly selected to be either a control (no change in instruction or materials) or the intervention (a change based on the researcher's question). Random assignment requires that any participant in the study have an equal chance of being assigned to any group. Chance alone determines placement (Ary, Jacobs, & Razavieh, 2002). Because random assignment is so difficult to achieve in schools, in part because of ethical restraints, most experiments are conducted in research labs.

For example, a researcher may want to know if a specific strategy such as thinking aloud will enhance first graders' comprehension. The researcher selects a multitude of first-grade classrooms throughout the country, thus ensuring that all kinds of children are represented in the study (e.g., wealthy and poor children, English language learners and those who have English as a native language, and so on). Then the researcher assesses the children in each class and children are restructured into classrooms based on the results of the preassessment measures. This restructuring is done so that children in each group are similar based on characteristics such as letter knowledge or reading ability. Once the classrooms are organized, the researcher instructs the teachers in how to use the think-aloud procedures with their students. Procedures are very specific and most often scripted, so there is no variation among teachers. The researcher is expected to check in with the teachers and make sure they use the strategy exactly as the researcher planned—treatment fidelity. After a specified amount of time, the researcher posttests all of the children in the experiment (both control and experimental groups) to determine if there are statistically significant differences between the two groups of children.

The researcher also evaluates effect sizes. Effect sizes let the researcher know that the intervention increased the childrens' learning by more than would happen just by their being in school and receiving typical instruction during the time of the experiment. For example, if a child demonstrates a year's growth in reading as measured by a standardized reading test at the end of an academic year, the intervention would not be considered a success. To be considered successful a child would need to demonstrate more than one year's growth during the academic year.

The strategy used in the intervention would only be considered research based *and* appropriate for use in first-grade classrooms if there were statistically significant differences between the control and experimental groups. However, researchers would want to see this study replicated so that there would be an accumulation of support for this strategy. Additionally, this study only considered first graders, so to be appropriate for second grade or other grades, other similar studies would need to be implemented.

The above fictional study would require extensive time and financial resources to carry out. The researcher would have to travel to each site numerous times and all of the pre- and postassessment data would need to be analyzed. Quality experimental research prefers to assess children or teachers and then place them in groups. Most schools and school districts disapprove of this practice because it is so disruptive and upsetting to parents, teachers, and students. This is why many true experimental studies are carried out in laboratory settings, rather than in classrooms.

Experimental studies do not appear frequently in our literacy research journals. Lomax (2004) investigated the design of articles in the two major literacy research journals (*Reading Research Quarterly* and *Journal of Literacy Research*) for the past five years to discover the number of experimental studies published. He found seventeen experimental studies. Of these seventeen, we chose one written by Calhoon and Leslie (2002) as an example that you might investigate. In this study, the researchers considered two variables (word frequency and rime) to explore young children's reading. See Table 2.1 for published examples of the research designs shared in this chapter.

Quasi-experimental designs lack random assignment. When a researcher uses this design, he or she uses classrooms or students that are available. The researcher typically matches students or classrooms based on specific variables. The goal of matching is to pair similar students or classrooms with one serving as the control and the other as the treatment (the group that receives the intervention). Researchers using this design are careful to assess differences in the groups and to use appropriate statistical techniques for these differences. Although quasi-experimental designs are not as pure as true experiments, they yield valuable information for educators. And when these designs are joined with other research endeavors, they contribute to strong research support for various strategies or materials.

Although there are many examples of quasi-experiments, we chose the work of Brown, Pressley, Van Meter, and Schuder (1996) as an example. In this study they compared students from five intact classrooms with students in five other classrooms. They studied the effects of using transactional comprehension strategies with students to increase comprehension.

Experiments are expensive to conduct. Pressley (2002) noted that after he conducted a quasi-experimental evaluation of transactional comprehension strategies (Brown, Pressley, Van Meter, & Schuder, 1996) and found that these strategies made a difference to students, he was not able to conduct other similar studies around these strategies. He stated, "The answer is that no follow up or replication

TABLE 2.1   Exemplary Studies for Each Research Design

Designs	Studies
Experimental	Calhoon, J., & Leslie, L. (2002). A longitudinal study of the effects of word frequency and rime-neighborhood size on beginning readers' rime reading accuracy in words and nonwords. *Journal of Literacy Research, 34,* 39–58.
Quasi-experimental	Brown, R., Pressley, M., Van Meter, P., & Schuder, T. (1996). A quasi-experimental validation of transactional strategies instruction with low-achieving second grade readers. *Journal of Educational Psychology, 88,* 18–37.
Correlational	Juel, C. (1988). Learning to read and write: A longitudinal study of 54 children from first through fourth grades. *Journal of Educational Psychology, 80,* 437–447.
Meta-analysis	Ehri, L., Nunes, S., Willows, D., Schuster, B., Yaghoub-Zadeh, Z., & Shanahan, T. (2001). Phonemic awareness instruction helps children learn to read: Evidence from the National Reading Panel's meta-analysis. *Reading Research Quarterly, 36,* 250–287.
Ethnography	Heath, S. B. (1983). *Ways with words: Language, life, and work in communities and classrooms.* Cambridge, MA: Cambridge University Press.
Case Study	Barone, D. (1999). *Resilient children: Stories of poverty, drug exposure, and literacy development.* Newark, DE: International Reading Association.
Cultural Studies	Jimenez, R., Smith, P., & Martinez-Leon, N. (2003). Freedom and form: The language and literacy practices of two Mexican schools. *Reading Research Quarterly, 38,* 488–509.
Historical Studies	Willis, A. (2002). Literacy at Calhoun Colored School 1892–1945. *Reading Research Quarterly, 37,* 8–45.

is planned. I simply do not have the resources to do such a study" (p. 35). He concluded that while replication studies are important, educators are going to have to make decisions on a few well-done studies in most cases, as research is so expensive to do experimentally.

Correlational studies.   Correlational studies are nonexperimental studies. Researchers have no control over who specifically participates in the treatment (McEwan & McEwan, 2003). An example of this type of study might be centered around district-wide literacy professional development workshops. The district decides they want to know if the professional development workshops have made a difference to student learning. Because not all of the teachers in the district attended the first workshop, only those that did are considered to be participants in the study. The researcher is limited to these teacher participants who may or may not be representative of all of the teachers in the district. The researcher tallies the workshops these teachers have attended and looks at the results of the criterion reference test to see if the students of these teachers had higher achievement than other classes in the district. The result might be that these teachers' students do score higher and thus the professional development is seen as having a positive effect on student achievement. Although this may be true, the researcher cannot assume that the professional development *caused* this result. Correlational studies only show that there was a relationship between the two, not that one caused the other. For example, it could be that all of the literacy leaders for this district attended the first workshop. These teachers, having more knowledge about effective ways to teach literacy, may have had higher student achievement scores before they attended the workshop. Knowing who the participants were in this research is very important to understanding the results.

Correlational studies often serve as an important research step that leads or does not lead to quasi-experimental or experimental studies. If a researcher's correlational study does not yield a statistically significant correlation, then there is no reason to move on to an experimental study. Pressley (2002) gives the example of how correlational studies on phonemic awareness led researchers to explore it experimentally. In 1988, Juel documented how children with high phonemic awareness in kindergarten were better readers in elementary school. This correlation led to experimental work by numerous other researchers (see Ehri et al., 2001).

There are certainly other quantitative designs; however experimental, quasi-experimental, and correlational designs are the most often used in educational research—especially work focused on literacy. Although these designs are the most frequent, teachers may also want to review metanalyses in which researchers have culled all of the studies in an area. Often metanalyses have very specific guidelines about which studies can be included. They offer teachers a way to see a rich body of evidence around a topic.

The National Reading Panel report (2000) qualifies as a metanalysis of studies in phonemic awareness, phonics, fluency, comprehension, and vocabulary. This panel limited the studies they considered to those that (a) addressed achievement with children from preschool to grade 12, (b) were generalizable to larger populations of students (used experimental or quasi-experimental designs), (c) examined the effectiveness of an approach, and (d) were regarded as high-quality by a peer-reviewed journal. (See www.nationalreadingpanel.org for more details about this report.) Another metanalysis was conducted by Ehri and colleagues (2001) on phonemic awareness instruction and how it supports learning to read.

Qualitative Studies

Qualitative research is also used to answer educational questions. This research tradition comes from anthropology (Schwandt, 1997). Qualitative research answers different questions than does quantitative research. Whereas quantitative research is seeking relationships, especially causal ones, qualitative research wants to know how and why something happens. This research design is focused on meaning. Qualitative research has three major characteristics:

1. The use of naturalistic settings in which researchers observe students in their classrooms or schools to learn about them as readers.
2. The researcher provides rich description about the phenomenon that is observed.
3. The research is centered on meaning or the interpretation of what is observed and documented.

Unlike quantitative research, in which researchers rely on assessments and statistical testing, qualitative researchers rely on observation, interviews, and artifacts. To gain trustworthiness for their research, they are at the research site for a considerable amount of time, they gain data from a variety of sources to seek convergence or dissonance in results or understandings, and they often include multiple voices (e.g., the teacher, student, parent) to gain a rich understanding of a phenomenon.

Ethnography.   One of the most classic qualitative designs is ethnography. This design is focused on learning about the culture of a group of people (LeCompte & Preissle, 1993). A researcher or group of researchers enters a location to discover and describe the culture, beliefs, values, and traditions of a group of people. Typically they stay at the site for a year or more. Because this design comes from anthropology most of us think about going to a far away location to study a group of people, similar to the work of Margaret Mead in New Guinea (1930), when we think of this design. However, educational researchers often study schools or classrooms to learn about how such cultures come to be and how they help or hinder students and teachers.

Ways with Words, a well-known ethnography centered on literacy, was conducted by Shirley Brice Heath (1983) for ten years. In this study she documented the home literacy traditions in three communities and how they supported or hindered children's success in school literacy learning. It continues to be a fascinating read for teachers today and a way to understand the great influence home, community, and society have on children's education.

Case studies.   Case study research is typically centered on a group or individual that is bounded in some way. *Bounded* is a label for defining what is to be studied and what is excluded (Stake, 2000). For example, a researcher may want to study one school that works with high-poverty children. In this case, the researcher would only study the principal, teachers, parents, other support staff, and students at this school to find answers to a guiding question. The question might be, "Why do students at this at-risk school test well in reading, when similar children at other schools do not test as well in reading?" As with ethnography, the researcher is typically at the site for a year or more to answer a guiding research question.

There are three different kinds of case studies according to Stake (1995). They include the *intrinsic case study,* in which the researcher is interested in learning about a specific case. The researcher may closely study one group of teachers as they participate in a learning community centered on comprehension, for example. The researcher is only interested in how this group works together and how they bring what they discuss to their classrooms. A second type is the *instrumental case study,* in which the researcher uses one case to understand a larger phenomenon. For example, the researcher may study one struggling reader to better understand the circumstances of other struggling readers. The last type is a *collective case study,* in which the researcher studies multiple cases concurrently. Through collective case study, the researcher can compare cases and note similarities and differences. Multiple cases allow the researcher to make claims to other similar groups. For instance, if several struggling readers are studied and the researcher observes that one-to-one prereading of a story helps with comprehension, then other teachers might also use this strategy with struggling readers based on multiple-case study reports.

There are many examples of case study research in journals and books. For an example, we have chosen Barone's work (1999) that explored the literacy development of children prenatally exposed to crack cocaine. She studied twenty-six children as they learned to read and write at home and at school and described their individual literacy development.

The story-like style of case studies and their practical applications make this a popular format for teachers to read and explore together. We recommend them for teacher study groups and for personal teacher writing as well.

Cultural studies.   Cultural studies investigate power relationships between groups. Researchers using this design often explore relationships that have gone unnoticed (Gall, Gall, & Borg, 2003). These researchers, through their work, are trying to change explicit circumstances that harm or disenfranchise teachers, parents, and students. Researchers using this design hold several assumptions, which include:

- Certain groups hold privileged status over other groups.
- Oppression has many forms, including gender, status, and other designations.
- Language is central to understanding relationships.
- Thought is mediated by power relationships that are socially and historically constructed.

Researchers in this tradition may study how a particular reading program benefits some children while it limits the possibilities for development of others. They might also study the informal curriculum and how it constrains students or teachers; for example, how a teacher's rule that only one child speak at a time may restrict the way some children typically engage in overlapping speech to understand a concept. These researchers may also study how new teachers are given the least desirable classroom with few materials to show how they are marginalized by colleagues within their new school setting.

An example of a cultural study is one conducted by Jimenez, Smith, and Martinez-Leon (2003). These researchers investigated the language and literacy practices of two elementary schools in Mexico to explore important differences between them and how they contributed to or hindered students' literacy growth.

Historical studies.   Historical research systematically examines past events to better understand current circumstances. Berg (1998) identified why this research is important: to uncover what was previously unknown or partially known, to answer questions, to identify a relationship between the past and present, to evaluate accomplishments, and to better understand our current culture.

Historical research requires researchers to seek out original documents from the past to support findings. Frequently diaries, newspaper articles, and textbooks serve as data. Nila Banton Smith's study of American reading instruction (2002) serves as a model of this research design. An example that appeared in a journal is one by Arlette Willis (2002), in which she studied literacy practices at Calhoun Colored School.

As with quantitative designs, there are certainly more qualitative designs than those described here. However, ethnography and case study are the most common designs used by educational researchers studying reading and writing.

How to Find Quality Research

As teachers we are faced with enormous challenges in choosing from a vast array of professional materials that are available to help us make decisions about the strategies and materials we use with students. Thankfully, there are guidelines that can help teachers find the most up to date and credible research tied to classroom practice.

Peer-Reviewed Journals

According to Stanovich (2003), "peer-reviewed journals provide a first pass filter that teachers can use to evaluate the plausibility of educational claims" (p. 7). The editors of peer-reviewed journals have policies to critically review manuscripts that are submitted for publication. First, they send the manuscript out for blind review to several reviewers who are experts in the topic and methodology of the study. The author of the work is not known to these reviewers. These experts write reviews of the manuscript noting strengths and weaknesses. Based on this feedback, the editors then reject the manuscript, ask the author(s) to revise it and return it for another round of reviews, ask the author(s) to revise it, or accept it as is for publication.

Most peer-reviewed journals are identified as such right in each journal. There are several literacy research journals that are peer reviewed. The ones that are most recognizable to a majority of teachers are *Reading Research Quarterly, Journal of Literacy Research,* and *Research in the Teaching of English.* There are other peer-reviewed journals that include literacy research along with other educational topics; these include *Elementary School Journal* and *Educational Researcher.*

There are peer-reviewed journals that make connections between theory and research and practice. These journals ask authors to translate their work for teachers and highlight the practice rather than the research design. Peer-reviewed teacher practitioner journals include *The Reading Teacher* and *Language Arts* for literacy. These journals are read more frequently by teachers because the connections to classroom practice are explicit and easily adapted for their students.

Non-Peer-Reviewed Journals

Not all journals for teachers and researchers are peer reviewed. Some of the most familiar journals for educators fall into this category. Authors submit manuscripts to the editors of these journals and editors decide whether to publish the work. They generally do not send the work out for reviewers' critical comments. Journals in this category include *The Kappan* and *Educational Leadership.*

Often these journals print opinions that may or may not be research based. Teachers are cautioned to check out the references at the end of these articles to find the research base for any strategy that is recommended.

Professional Magazines

There are many magazines that are written to support the day-to-day instructional practices of teachers. These include *The Mailbox, Teaching K–8, Teacher,* and *Instructor.* The strategies that are offered in these magazines may or may not be research supported. For teachers to make sure that a strategy offered is research supported, they will need to read the references that are provided at the end of an article. Teachers should look to see if the author of a particular article is citing his or her own research study or the studies of others to support the recommended strategy.

Professional Books

There are numerous professional books on the market to facilitate the work of teachers. Many professional books are sent out for review to experts in the field before they are published. The International Reading Association does this, as do other educational publishers like Allyn and Bacon, Guilford, Stenhouse, Heinemann, and others. This review process assures teachers that the strategies presented are research based. However, teachers must remember that an author is interpreting the research; in most cases the author was not the researcher.

Professional books generally fall into three categories: handbooks, edited books, and single- or multiple-authored books that could include textbooks. Handbooks are a compilation of all the research in certain areas. Each chapter is similar to a metanalysis of the research pertinent to an area. Some of the more familiar handbooks are *The Handbook of Reading Research* (Kamil, Mosenthal, Pearson,

& Barr, 2000), *The Handbook of Early Literacy Research* (Neuman & Dickinson, 2001), and *The Handbook of Research on Teaching the English Language Arts* (Flood, Lapp, Squire, & Jensen, 2003).

Edited books are another category of professional books for teachers. In these books, the editors generally look for experts to write each chapter of the book. A few examples of these types of books are: *No Quick Fix* (Allington & Walmsley, 1995), *Multicultural and Multilingual Literacy and Language* (Boyd & Brock, 2004), *Literacy in African American Communities* (Harris, Kamhi, & Pollock, 2001), *Teaching Reading* (Taylor & Pearson, 2002), and *Literacy and Young Children* (Barone & Morrow, 2003). The advantage of these books is that an expert, typically a researcher, is writing about the topic that he or she studies extensively.

Single- or multiple-authored professional books are typically focused on a topic for which the author synthesizes the research and theoretical work for the reader. There are a great variety of such books available for teachers. The following are just a few titles: *Change over Time in Children's Literacy Development* (Clay, 2001), *The Brothers and Sisters Learn to Write* (Dyson, 2003), *Learning to Read* (Pressley, Allington, Wharton-McDonald, Block, & Morrow, 2001), and *Assessment for Reading Instruction* (McKenna & Stahl, 2003).

Books play an important role for teachers as they discover and implement research-based practices. In 1997, Shanahan and Neuman searched literacy research to find the most significant work that influenced classroom practice. Their list of thirteen works included Atwell's *In the Middle* (1987), Clay's *Early Detection of Reading Difficulties* (1985), and Durkin's *Children Who Read Early* (1966).

Teachers need to consider all of this work as they search for research-based practices to implement with students. As they explore the research, they should consider objectivity in the work. Research conducted by publishers or developers of a product they sell or endorse is questionable, for instance. If other outside researchers find similar results, then the work is more objective and credible. Teachers are cautioned to consider the author of the research reports they read and note if the author is financially connected to a product they are investigating. In addition, teachers should look for converging evidence. When they find multiple reports written by different authors, they can have confidence in the findings. Teachers might also consider similar findings when done with a variety of research designs. For example, a scientist may discover through a qualitative investigation that think-alouds help comprehension. This study coupled with an experimental or quasi-experimental study builds confidence in the usefulness of this strategy.

How to Read Research Studies

Once you have located a research study that you think may have merit and possible use for a classroom, you need to read it carefully. Most research articles for education are organized following guidelines from the American Psychological Association. This organizational structure lets you know exactly where each important element of a study is placed. Research studies organized this way begin with an introduction, followed by a literature review that provides the theoretical grounding for the study, a careful and detailed method section, the results section, and finally a discussion section that ties the results back to the information synthesized in the literature review.

There are several questions that the reader should respond to as he or she evaluates the work that is reported. Table 2.2 shares these questions organized around each section of the research report.

In addition to these questions, which are focused directly on a research report, McEwan and McEwan (2003) caution teachers to respond to five other questions. These questions are centered around taking a research strategy and implementing it in a classroom.

1. The causal question: Does it work?
2. The process question: How does it work?

TABLE 2.2   Evaluating an Article

Section of Article	Questions
Introduction	What is the purpose of this study?
	Why is this work important?
	How does this work add to the knowledge base?
Literature review	Is the review up to date?
	Does the author present all views of this topic?
	Is the work that is shared synthesized and thoroughly presented?
	Does the work shared relate directly to this study?
Method	Is the research question clear?
	Are all the details of how this study was conducted shared?
	• Participants
	• Site of the study
	• Data collection
	• Data analysis
	Does the author share limitations of this study?
Results	Are the results clearly presented?
	For quantitative studies, are all the statistical results clearly explained? Does the author share effect sizes?
	For qualitative studies, is there enough data presented so that the results are credible?
Discussion	Does the discussion tie back to the literature review?
	Are the interpretations logically drawn from the results?

3. The cost question: Is it worthwhile?
4. The usability question: Will it work for me?
5. The evaluation question: Is it working for me? (p. 4)

They recommend that the first four questions be considered before adopting a program, method, or strategy.

Investigating the research pertinent to a strategy is time consuming. A teacher first needs to find an appropriate article or book that is focused on the chosen strategy or topic. Then he or she must critically read the text focusing on both the content and the credibility of the author. Finally, the teacher needs to consider this strategy and how it might work for the students for which he or she is responsible. We have found that this process is less onerous and lonely when teachers work together. For example, teachers at a certain grade level or within a school can identify a topic or strategy for study and then meet to share readings or talk about one that they have all read. Conversation following the critical reading is energizing because it helps teachers work together to facilitate student learning in their classrooms and school.

Practical Support for Teachers

Although going to the original research is the best way to guarantee that a strategy or program is research based, there are other supports that also help teachers determine this. The International Reading Association, in partnership with the National Council of Teachers of English, has created a website called *Read.Write.Think* (www.readwritethink.org). This website is organized around lessons in learning language, learning about language, and learning through language. The lessons cover the important topics of fluency, comprehension, vocabulary, word study, content reading, critical literacy, writing, and more. They are also grouped by grades (K–12).

All of the lessons have been written by teachers to specific requirements. For example, we selected a learning language activity for K–2 students. The lesson begins with an overview of the generating rhymes lesson that targets phonemic awareness. Following this synopsis is an article link with research that supports the activity. Each activity identifies the IRA/NCTE standards that are addressed. To further support teachers, all the objectives of the lesson are identified along with a detailed instructional plan. Within each plan any resource that might be needed is identified. In this lesson, the poem *Down by the Bay* is printed along with a rhyming packet of worksheets. The lesson ends with assessment activities.

All of the lessons are structured in a similar manner. For some, there are links to websites to facilitate learning. For example, in a lesson about the book *Corduroy* there is a link to a complete CIMC Integrated Unit that centers on *Corduroy*. There is also a link to a biography of the author, Don Freeman.

The key to each of these lessons is the link to a research article that supports each strategy. Teachers can be assured that the lessons provided are research based.

In addition, teachers can print the article and use it in discussions with other teachers, parents, or their principal.

Research-Based Programs

In addition to using research based practices, Reading First legislation expects that schools and teachers will use research-based core programs for instruction. In fact, only programs that schools and teachers have determined to be research-based for use in Reading First schools are funded. To assure this, schools and districts are examining their core programs to see their strengths and limitations in meeting the expectations for scientifically based reading materials. This process is challenging because each book from a core series must be evaluated to see how it supports the teaching of phonemic awareness, phonics, and so on at each grade level. In addition to determining how these literacy elements are taught at each grade level, there is an expectation that there is continual support for each element throughout the elementary grades.

Edward Kame'enui and colleagues have created a consumer's guide to materials (www.opi.state.mt.us/pdf/ReadingEx/ConsumerGuide.pdf) that facilitates the critical evaluation of core programs. They ask an evaluator to consider the following questions:

- Are there experimental studies to support the effectiveness of the core program?
- Does the program reflect current and confirmed research in reading?

Following these broad questions, the evaluator must determine if there is explicit and systematic instruction in grades K–3 of phonemic awareness (K–1), phonics, decoding, word recognition, spelling, vocabulary, comprehension, writing, and oral and written language. The last question targets the core program to the students in schools that are similar to the one in which the program is being evaluated. Kame'enui and colleagues ask for evidence that children similar to the ones in this school have learned to read effectively with this core program. The consumer's guide then targets each element at each grade level for further evaluation. Figure 2.1 shares a part of a page of this guide so you can get an idea of the depth of expectations for each element.

This analysis continues for each element and for each grade throughout the primary grades. At the end of the analysis, teachers and schools know whether their program is scientifically based and in what ways it does not meet the explicit and systematic expectations for instruction.

Teachers might also choose another format to investigate their core program. Figure 2.2 shares a format tied to each literacy component and how it is used at each grade level.

As teachers, we understand that this is not an easy process to complete. It can take days or weeks to complete this thorough analysis. Not surprising to most teachers, publishers have completed the Kame'enui evaluation for their core

FIGURE 2.1   A Portion of the Consumer Guide

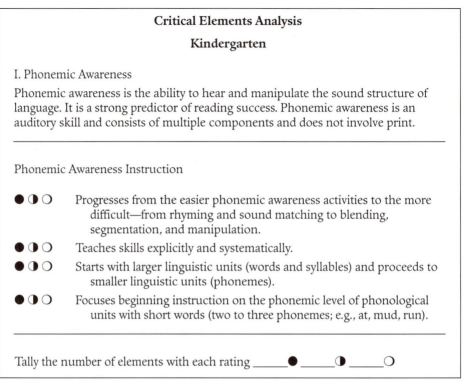

Critical Elements Analysis

Kindergarten

I. Phonemic Awareness

Phonemic awareness is the ability to hear and manipulate the sound structure of language. It is a strong predictor of reading success. Phonemic awareness is an auditory skill and consists of multiple components and does not involve print.

Phonemic Awareness Instruction

● ◑ ○   Progresses from the easier phonemic awareness activities to the more difficult—from rhyming and sound matching to blending, segmentation, and manipulation.

● ◑ ○   Teaches skills explicitly and systematically.

● ◑ ○   Starts with larger linguistic units (words and syllables) and proceeds to smaller linguistic units (phonemes).

● ◑ ○   Focuses beginning instruction on the phonemic level of phonological units with short words (two to three phonemes; e.g., at, mud, run).

Tally the number of elements with each rating _____ ● _____ ◑ _____ ○

programs. Although we encourage schools and teachers to consider the publishers' completed evaluations, we caution them not to rely only on these evaluations. Publishers tend to present their programs as doing an exemplary job with each literacy element at all grade levels. Although published programs are certainly paying more attention to the literacy elements, no program is perfect. We have found that as teachers collaboratively engage in the critical evaluation of their core programs, they identify when elements like comprehension or vocabulary need to be supplemented to reach the needs of students in their schools.

Conclusion

The expectations for classroom instruction and materials have changed with the No Child Left Behind legislation, particularly Reading First. Teachers can no longer choose a strategy or core text that they think might benefit the learning expectations and needs of their students. They are now expected to know and understand the current research base centered on literacy instruction, know how to systematically and explicitly teach this content to their students, and understand how to evaluate the core texts they use to determine their scientific base.

FIGURE 2.2   **Evaluating a Core Program**

Literacy Element	Strategies (List strategies that are suggested. Are they current? Are they sufficient?)	Grade Level
Phonemic Awareness		
Phonics		
Comprehension		
Fluency		
Vocabulary		

These expectations are not easy to accomplish. They are challenging and time consuming. Moreover, they are expectations placed on top of the already challenging job of teaching. Because of this challenge, we recommend that teachers work together with their principal, district, and parents to explore the scientific research and determine which practices are best for the children at their schools. Through these collaborative efforts, teachers will understand how to facilitate the development of students who can read and write and who enjoy doing so.

References

Allington, R., & Walmsley, S. (Eds.). (1995). *No quick fix: Rethinking literacy programs in America's elementary schools.* Newark, DE: International Reading Association.

Ary, D., Jacobs, L., & Razavieh, A. (2002). *Introduction to research in education* (6th ed.). Belmont, CA: Wadsworth Publishing.

Atwell, N. (1987). *In the middle.* Portsmouth, NH: Heinemann.

Barone, D. (1999). *Resilient children: Stories of poverty, drug exposure, and literacy development.* Newark, DE: International Reading Association.

Barone, D., & Morrow, L. (Eds.). (2003). *Literacy and young children.* New York: Guilford.

Berg, B. (1998). *Qualitative research methods for the social sciences.* Boston: Allyn and Bacon.

Boyd, F., & Brock, C. (2004). *Multicultural and multilingual literacy and language.* New York: Guilford.

Brown, R., Pressley, M., Van Meter, P., & Schuder, T. (1996). A quasi-experimental validation of transactional strategies instruction with low-achieving second grade readers. *Journal of Educational Psychology, 88,* 18–37.

Calhoon, J., & Leslie, L. (2002). A longitudinal study of the effects of word frequency and rime-neighborhood size on beginning readers' rime reading accuracy in words and nonwords. *Journal of Literacy Research, 34,* 39–58.

Clay, M. (1985). *The early detection of reading difficulties.* Auckand, New Zealand: Heinemann.

Clay, M. (2001). *Change over time in children's literacy development.* Portsmouth, NH: Heinemann.

Durkin, D. (1966). *Children who read early.* New York: Teachers College Press.

Dyson, A. (2003). *The brothers and sisters learn to write.* New York: Teachers College Press.

Ehri, L., Nunes, S., Willows, D., Schuster, B., Yaghoub-Zadeh, Z., & Shanahan, T. (2001). Phonemic awareness instruction helps children learn to read: Evidence from the National Reading Panel's meta-analysis. *Reading Research Quarterly, 36,* 250–287.

Flood, J., Lapp, D., Squire, J., & Jensen, J. (Eds.). (2003). *Handbook of research on teaching the English language arts* (2nd ed.). Mahwah, NJ: Erlbaum.

Gall, M., Gall, J., & Borg, W. (2003). *Educational research: An introduction* (7th ed.). Boston: Allyn and Bacon.

Harris, J., Kamhi, A., & Pollock, K. (Eds.). (2001). *Literacy in African American communities.* Mahwah, NJ: Erlbaum.

Heath, S. B. (1983). *Ways with words: Language, life, and work in communities and classrooms.* Cambridge, MA: Cambridge University Press.

Jimenez, R., Smith, P., & Martinez-Leon, N. (2003). Freedom and form: The language and literacy practices of two Mexican schools. *Reading Research Quarterly, 38,* 488–509.

Juel, C. (1988). Learning to read and write: A longitudinal study of 54 children from first through fourth grades. *Journal of Educational Psychology, 80,* 437–447.

Kamil, M. (2004). The current state of quantitative research. *Reading Research Quarterly, 39,* 100–107.

Kamil, M., Mosenthal, P., Pearson, P. D., & Barr, R. (Eds.). (2000). *Handbook of reading research* (Vol. 3). Mahwah, NJ: Erlbaum.

LeCompte, M., & Preissle, J. (1993). *Ethnography and qualitative design in educational research.* San Diego, CA: Academic Press.

Lomax, R. (2004). Whither the future of quantitative literacy research? *Reading Research Quarterly, 39,* 107–112.

McEwan, E., & McEwan, P. (2003). *Making sense of research: What's good, what's not, and how to tell the difference.* Thousand Oaks, CA: Corwin Press.

McKenna, M., & Stahl, S. (2003). *Assessment for reading instruction.* New York: Guilford.

McMillan, J. H., & Wergin, J. F. (2002) *Understanding and evaluating education research* (2nd ed.). Upper Saddle River, NJ: Pearson.

Mead, M. (1930). *Growing up in New Guinea: A comparative study of primitive education.* New York: William Morrow.

National Reading Panel (NRP). (2000). *Teaching children to read: An evidence-based assessment of the scientific research literature on reading and its implications for reading instruction.* Washington, DC: National Institute of Child Health and Human Development.

Neuman, S., & Dickinson, D. (Eds.). (2001). *Handbook of early literacy research.* New York: Guilford.

Pressley, M. (2002). What I have learned up until now about research methods in reading instruction. In D. Schallert, C. Faribanks, J. Worthy, B. Maloch, & J. Hoffman (Eds.), *51st yearbook of the National Reading Conference* (pp. 33–45). Oak Creek, WI: National Reading Conference.

Pressley, M., Allington, R., Wharton-McDonald, R., Block, C., & Morrow, L. (2001). *Learning to read: Lessons from exemplary first-grade classrooms.* New York: Guilford.

Schwandt, T. (1997). *Qualitative inquiry: A dictionary of terms.* Thousand Oaks, CA: Sage.

Shanahan, T., & Neuman, S. (1997). Conversations: Literacy research that makes a difference. *Reading Research Quarterly, 32,* 202–211.

Smith, N. (2002). *American reading instruction* (Special ed.). Newark, DE: International Reading Association.

Snow, C., Burns, M., & Griffin, P. (Eds.). (1998). *Preventing reading difficulties in young children.* Washington, DC: National Academy Press.

Stake, R. (1995). *The art of case study research.* Thousand Oaks, CA: Sage.

Stake, R. (2000). Case studies. In N. Denzin & Y. Lincoln (Eds.), *Handbook of qualitative research* (2nd ed., pp. 435–454). Thousand Oaks, CA: Sage.

Stanovich, K. (2003). *Using research and reason in education.* Washington, DC: National Institute for Literacy.

Taylor, B., & Pearson, P. D. (Eds.). (2002). *Teaching reading.* Mahwah, NJ: Erlbaum.

United States Department of Education. (2003). *Inside No Child Left Behind.* Retrieved March 25, 2003, from http://www.ed.gov/legislation/ESEA02/pg2.html#sec119.

Willis, A. (2002). Literacy at Calhoun Colored School 1892–1945. *Reading Research Quarterly, 37,* 8–45.

chapter three

What Are the Essential Components of Reading Instruction?

At end of the summer months, Sarah and Ellen each attend separate Reading First Academies presented by their state and district. Ellen is reaffirmed by listening to some of the practices she has used with her third graders and is interested in some of the new comprehension strategies that are shared. Some are very much like approaches she has used in the past, but discarded for reasons now beyond her memory. She is pretty sure it was not because they were not useful; instead, there may have been some newer ideas or programs she was interested in trying. In any case, it is like becoming reacquainted with an old friend.

Sarah gathers information and ideas for next year's plans and now understands why she was so overwhelmed last year. Teaching first graders to read, she realizes, is a very complex task. Although she now has a good understanding of the key elements, she's wondering how to put them all together in a logical, well-ordered format to present to her students.

As the new school year approaches, Ellen and Sarah are organizing and planning content in all the subject areas, revising classroom management procedures and schedules, and rearranging classroom space, knowing full well that until they actually meet their students, certain aspects will need to stay flexible and some will necessarily remain permanent. And they are thoughtfully planning how they will meet the literacy needs of all of their students by using the new strategies that they learned about in their Reading First Academies.

The legislation behind Reading First defines five essential components of reading instruction based on the report from the National Reading Panel (NRP). The NRP report *Teaching Children to Read: An Evidenced-Based Assessment of the Scientific Research Literature on Reading and Its Implications for Reading Instruction* (2000) has a major impact on states, districts, schools, and classroom teachers. Although there is considerable debate over how the Panel selected studies to include in their report and how to interpret the set of studies included, the report is an extensive metanalysis that includes a broad range of studies organized around the following five major topics:

1. *Phonemic awareness.* The ability to hear, identify, and manipulate the individual sounds (phonemes) in spoken words.
2. *Phonics.* The relationship between the letters used in written language and the sounds of spoken language.
3. *Fluency.* The ability to read quickly and accurately with expression and understanding.
4. *Vocabulary.* Knowing and understanding the words used in oral and written language.
5. *Comprehension.* The ability to understand what has been read.

Although the components are described individually, they should be considered parts of a complete and comprehensive reading program. In other words, no single component is sufficient to teach children to read. In the same respect, all of the components are important and none should be left out.

Results from the NRP (2000) findings indicate that systematic and explicit instruction in the essential components is necessary to a comprehensive reading program. Systematic instruction means teaching based on a prescribed sequence of elements. For example, most phonics programs sequence the letter–sound patterns that are taught (as opposed to randomly selecting patterns or selecting patterns that appear in texts students are reading). In this instance, initial consonant sounds might be taught before consonant digraphs (e.g., *sh, th, ch*) and short vowels might be taught before vowel diphthongs (e.g., *oi* or *ou*). Explicit instruction means directly teaching a skill or strategy. Teachers explicitly instruct children on how to derive the meanings of words based on context (as opposed to letting children discover this on their own). Key to the panel's findings is the notion that children should be directly taught skills and strategies that have been organized in a logical order so that children progress from simple to more complex skills.

Although highly influential in contributing to the research community, the NRP is not the only source of research that can assist teachers. Many researchers and professional organizations have contributed significantly to the field. The National Reading Council's *Preventing Reading Difficulties in Young Children* (Snow, Burns, & Griffin, 1998) was organized by the National Research Council of the National Academy of Sciences at the request of the U.S. Department of Health and Human Services. This committee of child development experts was organized to determine what is known from the research on reading. Other organizations have contributed to our understanding of reading research, including the International Reading Association, the Center for the Improvement of Early Reading Achievement, the U.S. Department of Education, and the National Institute for Literacy.

Suggested Reading on Scientifically Based Reading Research

Farstrup, A. E., & Samuels, S. J. (Eds.). (2001). *What research has to say about reading instruction* (3rd ed.). Newark, DE: International Reading Association.

International Reading Association. (2002). *What is evidence-based reading instruction? A position statement of the international reading association.* Retrieved February 15, 2004, from http://www.reading.org/pdf/1055.pdf.

Snow, C. E., Burns, M. S., & Griffin, P. (1998). *Preventing reading difficulties in young children.* Washington, DC: National Academy Press.

Research in literacy helps answer questions about how children learn to read and provides valuable insight about what methods work for the different children in your classroom. There is no single best approach to teach children to read. However, there is a body of knowledge about a wide range of instructional methods that work with most children. Understanding these methods will help teachers match the right methods and materials with the students in their classrooms. It will also help steer teachers away from methods and materials that do not work. It takes qualified and talented teachers to use research-based information to craft the best reading instruction for all children.

This chapter is designed to be a user-friendly and practical guide for understanding the essential components of reading instruction. We provide information about each of the essential components as well as classroom instruction that supports literacy development based on research findings. The chapter also includes information that supports teachers in finding and using instructional materials and core reading programs. It is impossible to provide an in-depth discussion of each essential component. Therefore, we have provided suggested readings that will enhance your understanding of each essential component.

Phonemic Awareness

Phonemes are the smallest units of sound in spoken words. The word *top* has three phonemes: /t/ /o/ /p/. The word *ship* also has three phonemes: /sh/ /i/ /p/. The NRP (2000) defines phonemic awareness as "the ability to focus on and manipulate phonemes in spoken words" (p. 2-1). Many teachers confuse the terms *phonemic awareness* and *phonological awareness*. Phonological awareness is the understanding of the many ways spoken language can be divided, including sentences into words, words into syllables, onset and rime, and individual sounds (or phonemes) in words, syllables, onsets, and rimes. As you can see, phonemic awareness is a subset of phonological awareness.

To understand the importance of phonemic awareness in learning to read, you need to understand the importance of being able to hear and manipulate sounds in spoken words. Learning to read and write requires the learner to apply what he or she knows about spoken language to written language. Children need to understand that language is made up of words, words are made up of individual sounds, and that the individual sounds in spoken words are matched by the sequence of letters in written words.

Phonemic awareness is *not* phonics. However, it does help the learner make connections between the sounds of spoken language and the letter combinations used to represent those sounds. Without this basic understanding, it is difficult for young children to figure out how the alphabet works.

What Research Says about Phonemic Awareness

Phonemic awareness is the strongest predictor of success in learning to read (Adams, 1990). Helping children become phonemically aware significantly accelerates their reading and writing development (Ball & Blachman, 1991; Torgesen & Mathes, 1998). Children who lack phonemic awareness do not benefit fully from phonics instruction because they don't understand how the letters and sounds work (Juel, Griffith, & Gough, 1986; Snow, Burns, & Griffin, 1998). The NRP (2000) found that teaching children how to identify and manipulate the sounds in spoken words helps them learn to read and spell. The Panel also found that phonemic awareness instruction

- Improves children's understanding of how spoken words are represented in print
- Helps young children learn to decode and spell words

- Is most effective when children are taught to use letters to represent phonemes
- Is more effective when taught in small groups rather than one-on-one or as a whole group because children benefit from listening to their peers and having more opportunities to participate
- Is most effective when it closely matches the types of reading and spelling of emergent readers and writers
- Is most effective when taught explicitly and regularly

Phonemic Awareness in the Classroom

Because phonemic awareness relies heavily on understanding oral language, the classroom should be a rich environment where children are engaged in oral language. Children need to have ample opportunities to discuss, ask questions, and develop their oral language. They should participate in lively discussions, sing songs, chant familiar rhymes, and play with new and interesting words. Classroom instruction focuses on helping children make connections between their expanding oral language and their emerging understanding of written language.

Because phonemic awareness helps children make connections between oral language and written text, children also need to engage in reading and writing experiences that promote their emerging literacy. Children listen to a variety of stories and other texts read aloud to them. They engage in *pretend* reading by handling books, looking at pictures, and telling stories from the pictures in books. They also engage in *pretend* writing experiences by scribbling and drawing pictures, using letter-like forms, and writing important words such as their names and favorite locations (e.g., McDonalds, Target, Toys "R" Us).

Although some children learn phonological awareness on their own when engaged in the activities listed above, many children do not because they lack the early oral language and literacy experiences that promote phonological awareness. These children need a systematic and explicit program in order to develop this important concept. Teachers should explicitly and systematically teach the following phonemic awareness concepts:

- *Phoneme isolation*—recognizing individual sounds in a word such as the sound /m/ in the word *man.*
- *Phoneme identification*—identifying the common sounds in different words such as the sound /t/ in the words *toy, top,* and *tell.*
- *Phoneme categorization*—grouping words with similar sounds such as the /g/ sound in the words *rag, bug,* and *flag.*
- *Phoneme blending*—grouping a series of sounds into a word such as the sounds /k/ /a/ /t/ in the word *cat.*
- *Phoneme segmentation*—tapping out, counting, or saying the individual sounds in a word such as the /s/ /a/ /k/ sounds in the word *sack.*
- *Phoneme deletion*—identifying what word remains when a phoneme is deleted such as the word *lip* is the word *flip* without the /f/.

- *Phoneme manipulation*—substituting the sounds of a word to create a new word such as dropping the sound /p/ in the word *pig* and replacing it with the sound /b/ to make the word *big*.

Teachers are encouraged to focus on one concept during a lesson. It may be very confusing for children to focus on two elements (such as segmentation and deletion) in the same lesson. Teachers begin with those concepts that are simpler, such as phoneme isolation, before moving to more complex tasks such as phoneme manipulation. When possible, associate letters with sounds so that children begin to make connections between what they hear in oral language and the written representation of those sounds.

Many teachers wonder who needs phonemic awareness instruction and when should it begin. Honig, Diamond, and Gutlohn (2000) suggest the following:

- Begin phonemic awareness instruction in mid-kindergarten and continue throughout the early elementary grades as needed.
- Generally, once children demonstrate decoding abilities they are phonemically aware and no longer need formal instruction.
- Older children who are poor readers or nonreaders may need phonemic awareness instruction.
- Intervention for older students should involve frequent, intensive sessions, with practice focused on hearing the differences of the phonemes, along with blending exercises that associate sounds with spellings.

In addition, children who are able to invent spellings are no longer in need of phonemic awareness instruction. Children who represent sounds in written words with letters demonstrate an understanding of phonemes. Consider the example in Figure 3.1 from a kindergarten student. This child is able to segment each sound in the words she writes and represent those sounds with letters. Although the spelling is not conventional, it demonstrates that this child is phonemically aware.

The overall structure of an effective phonemic awareness program includes introducing, practicing, extending, and revisiting the various phonemic awareness

FIGURE 3.1   Young Child's Spelling

(I like my mom's new car)

tasks (Adams, Foorman, Lundberg, & Beeler, 1998). Individual lessons should be brief, yet allow children ample time to practice the individual skills. Yopp and Yopp (2000) suggest three important factors to keep in mind for phonemic awareness instruction in the classroom. First, activities must be child appropriate. Because phonemic awareness instruction is most beneficial for children who are emerging into literacy, songs, chants, word games, word play, nursery rhymes, story telling, rhymes, riddles, and overall playful and engaging activities are most appropriate. Second, phonemic awareness instruction should be deliberate and purposeful. Although some children may develop phonemic awareness incidentally by engaging in many of the activities listed above, children need to have direct and intentional instruction on the various concepts. Third, phonemic awareness instruction is only one part of a comprehensive literacy program. Unless placed within a context of learning to read and write, phonemic awareness instruction alone is unlikely to promote overall literacy development (Griffith & Olsen, 1992).

There are many commercial programs focused on phonological awareness for classroom use. However, two books have been published that outline highly effective, explicit, sequential, and research-based programs. *Phonemic Awareness in Young Children: A Classroom Curriculum* (Adams, Foorman, Lundberg, & Beeler, 1998) is a comprehensive curriculum that includes assessments and instructional activities that can be incorporated into classroom program in fifteen to twenty minutes a day. Activities focus on simple listening games and exercises in rhyming, alliteration, and segmentation. *Road to the Code: A Phonological Awareness Program for Young Children* (Blachman, Ball, Black, & Tangle, 2000) is a comprehensive curriculum for kindergartners and first graders who are having difficulties. This eleven-week program focuses on developing phonemic awareness and letter–sound correspondences. Detailed lessons and reproducible materials are included in both books.

Phonemic Awareness Checklist

Understanding that spoken words can be broken up into individual sounds does not come naturally for all children. Identifying the phonemes in a word can be difficult for many adults and equally confusing for five-year-old children. Phonemic awareness research can be translated into classroom practices that promote phonemic awareness and overall reading achievement. The following list is particularly helpful for kindergarten and first-grade teachers. Special education teachers and teachers of older children who are experiencing difficulty learning to read and write will find the checklist helpful as well. The classroom teacher who promotes phonemic awareness

- Provides ample opportunities for children to discuss, ask questions, and develop their oral language
- Encourages children to participate in lively discussions, sing songs, chant familiar rhymes, and play with new and interesting words
- Engages children in reading and writing experiences that promote their emergent literacy
- Teaches children to segment, blend, and manipulate sounds in oral language
- Has children clapping to count syllables in words

- Teaches children to hear and manipulate sounds in words (rhymes and plays with words)
- Monitors the growth and development of phonemic awareness of individual children
- Encourages children to explore new words
- Connects letters to phonemic awareness lessons and activities
- Uses *no* workbook pages, flashcard drills, endless trace-the-alphabet dittos, or nonauthentic literacy activities

Suggested Reading on Phonemic Awareness

Adams, M. J., Foorman, B. R., Lundberg, I., & Beeler, T. (1998). *Phonemic awareness in young children: A classroom curriculum.* Baltimore, MD: Paul H. Brooks.

Blachman, B. A., Ball, E. W., Black, R., & Tangle, D. M. (2000). *Road to the code: A phonological awareness program for young children.* Baltimore, MD: Paul H. Brooks.

Yopp, H. K., & Yopp, R. H. (2000). Supporting phonemic awareness development in the classroom. *The Reading Teacher, 54,* 130–143.

Phonics

Phonics is defined by *The Literacy Dictionary* (Harris & Hodges, 1995) as "a way of teaching reading and spelling that stresses symbol–sound relationships, used especially in beginning instruction" (p. 186). Phonics instruction plays a critical role in early literacy acquisition because it provides beginning readers with an understanding of the code used in written language, allowing them to decode and spell words. The NRP (2000) states that the purpose of phonics instruction is to help children "acquire knowledge of the alphabetic system and its use to decode new words and to recognize familiar words accurately and automatically" (p. 2-90). This means that children will understand the alphabetic principle—the notion that the sequence of letters in written words represents the sequence of sounds (or phonemes) in spoken words.

The Literacy Dictionary (Harris & Hodges, 1995) also identifies two major types of phonics instruction:

1. "Analytic phonics instruction—a whole-to-part approach to word study in which the student is first taught a number of sight words and then relevant phonic generalizations, which are subsequently applied to other words" (p. 9)
2. "Synthetic phonics—a part-to-whole approach to reading instruction in which the student learns the sounds represented by letters and letter combinations, blends these sounds to pronounce words, and finally identifies which phonic generalizations apply" (p. 250)

The NRP notes that a hallmark of systematic phonics programs is that they "delineate a planned, sequential set of phonic elements and they teach these elements explicitly and systematically" (2000, p. 2-91).

What Research Says about Phonics

Stanovich (1994) states that "direct instruction in alphabetic coding facilitates early reading acquisition is one of the most well-established conclusions in all of behavioral science" (p. 285). Chall (1967) found substantial evidence that systematic phonics improved word recognition, spelling, vocabulary, and reading comprehension. Like Chall, Adams (1990) found direct instruction in phonics to be one of the characteristics of exemplary teachers. However, Adams also stressed the importance of exposure to a lot of reading materials beyond the direct teaching of phonics. Although there are many ways to teach phonics, the NRP (2000) found that systematic and explicit phonics instruction better promotes children's reading and spelling development than alternative, nonsystematic programs or no phonics at all. Phonics instruction was found to be most effective when it was introduced as soon as children began learning to read, and lasted approximately two to three years. The effects of phonics instruction lasted beyond the training period. In addition, the NRP found that:

• Systematic phonics is most effective in kindergarten and first grade, or before children have learned to read independently.

• Phonics instruction is more effective than nonphonics approaches for younger children who are at risk of developing future reading problems, and in helping to remediate some older struggling readers.

• Systematic phonics instruction has an impact on comprehension, decoding, word reading, and spelling.

• Phonics instruction is most effective when taught individually, in small groups, and with the whole class.

Phonics in the Classroom

Teaching children the letters and sounds is not enough to produce a full understanding of the alphabetic system. Comprehensive phonics instruction provides a full range of letter–sound correspondences, including but not limited to:

• Consonant letters and sounds
• Vowel letters and sounds (short and long)
• Consonant blends
• Vowel and consonant digraphs
• Phonograms/word families (such as the -*an* family in the words *can, man,* and *fan*)

In addition to complete coverage of the above items, children need assistance with decoding strategies that involve sounding out words, blending letters to pronounce words, and segmenting sounds in words to spell.

Instruction should begin in preschool and kindergarten with letter knowledge, including recognizing, naming, and writing the letters of the alphabet. Most children will learn letter names before they learn letter sounds and they find it easier to learn the sound for each letter if they already have a name for it (Hall & Moats, 1999). Letter recognition includes identifying and distinguishing both up-percase and lowercase letters. The child who is thoroughly familiar with all of the letter names will have a much easier time associating sounds with letters since most of the names of letters are closely related to the sound they represent (Adams, 1990). To illustrate this point, get your mouth ready to say the name of this letter: *R*. Next, make the sound associated with that letter. Notice the position of your tongue and the shape of your lips. Both the name of the letter and the sound rep-resented by that letter involve the similar lip and tongue placement.

Teachers often wonder if there is a specific sequence to teach the sounds. Al-though there is no research to support a specific sequence, it stands to reason that you should teach the most frequently used letters and sounds first. Begin with let-ters and sounds that are most frequently used in the words children will encounter in the texts they read and write. Many programs focus on teaching letters that have a high utility for spelling simple, monosyllabic words. Adams, Foorman, Lundberg, and Beeler (1998) suggest beginning with the consonants *s, m, d, p, t, n, g, b, r, f,* and *l,* and the short vowels *a, o, i, u,* and *e*.

Beginning with a few consonants and a short vowel, children can learn to spell and decode a number of words right away. Continued work with these letters will quickly lead to children mastering some simple spelling patterns. Common spelling patterns are known as *phonograms* or *rimes* (e.g., *at, on*). Words that share the same spelling pattern are referred to as *word families* (e.g., *hat, bat, fat*).

The patterns children are exposed to when studying phonograms and word families will help them decode and spell many new words. Decoding and spelling by analogy help students associate words with sound or spelling patterns that they already know from other known words. They can apply this knowledge to read and spell unknown words. When writing, a child might want to use the word *smart* but doesn't know how to spell it. She or he might recall the *-art* spelling pattern from the word *cart* (a known word) and the *sm-* spelling pattern from the word *small* (a known word). By using these known elements, the child can figure out the spelling of an unknown word by associating it with known words. Through the use of analogies, beginning readers can build on their understanding of many spelling patterns to construct unknown words.

Teaching children to identify and spell words by analogy requires explicit teacher modeling. Teachers should encourage children to ask, "What words do I know that look the same?" and "What words do I know that contain the same spelling pattern?" Cunningham (2000) estimates that by teaching thirty-seven of the most common spelling patterns (such as *-ack, -un* and *-ump*), children will learn to spell over 500 of the most commonly used words in their reading and writing.

A plethora of commercial phonics programs are available for classroom use. Systematic programs should include a carefully selected and useful set of letter–sound relationships that are organized and introduced in a logical sequence. The program should introduce simple concepts such as initial consonant sounds, final consonant sounds, and short vowels before moving to consonant blends, long vowel patterns, and consonant and vowel digraphs.

We know that children enter classrooms with varying amounts of phonics knowledge. Some children enter a kindergarten classroom knowing a few letters and sounds. Some enter with a full understanding of how to decode words while reading. Others have little or no letter knowledge. Clearly, one phonics program will not meet the needs of all of these children. It is important that any phonics program include comprehensive assessment tools as well as guidelines for flexible instructional grouping.

Careful attention should be given to helping children apply letter–sound relationships as they relate to other areas of literacy instruction. When possible, letter–sound knowledge should be included in phonemic awareness instruction so that children understand the relationships between the sounds they hear in spoken words and the sequence of letters in words they read and write. Letter–sound relationships and spelling patterns should also be emphasized in all reading and writing experiences. Phonics can even be emphasized during vocabulary development. Children are eager to understand the relationship between the way we spell the word *health* and its derivation from the word *heal,* for example.

A Note on Decodable Texts

Decodable texts are texts that are written using a high percentage of words with letter–sound relationships that children have learned. There is considerable debate over the use of decodable texts. Many researchers (Beck, 1997; Kame'enui & Simmons, 1997; Jenkins, Vadasy, Peyton, & Sanders, 2003) have concluded that decodable texts are an essential part of the early reading curriculum. Decodable texts offer children opportunities to encounter words with spelling patterns that they are studying during phonics lessons. Exposure to these words in text reinforces the connection between phonics instruction and reading, allowing children to use their new phonics knowledge in reading-connected text. Some of these researchers have concluded that the vast majority of texts read by beginning readers should be decodable. Other researchers (Allington & Woodside-Jiron, 1998; Yatvin, Weaver, & Garan, 2003) find little or no value in using decodable texts. These researchers note that there is no scientific research that supports their use. They caution that many decodable texts don't make sense. The tightly controlled language patterns do not match the linguistic styles that authors use in writing children's books and they do not always follow the linguistic patterns children hear in oral language. This makes it very difficult for children to comprehend what is often nonsensical text. Still other researchers (Hiebert, 1999) find a middle ground in this debate. They note the importance of supporting the letter–sound patterns children learn in phonics in the texts that children read. Although the exact contributions of decodable texts are yet to be discovered, they can supplement the texts that children read in the classroom. Teachers might be best advised to include decodable texts as part of their phonics instruction. However, decodable texts should be a small supplement to high-quality reading materials, they should be highly interesting, and they must be comprehensible to young readers.

Phonics instruction should provide children with an understanding of why they are learning the relationships between letters and sounds as well as opportunities for them to practice the phonic patterns they are learning. There should be ample time for children to transfer their new knowledge of phonic patterns to the words, sentences, and texts they read and write. The NRP (2000) clearly states that "phonics is a means to an end" (p. 2-88) and that programs that place too much emphasis on learning phonics and not enough on putting phonics strategies to use in reading and writing are unlikely to be very effective.

Phonics Checklist

Systematic and explicit phonics instruction involves directly teaching sound–spelling patterns systematically. This type of instruction moves children from simple to more complex phonic concepts, allowing them to continually build on what they learn. It is not necessary to teach every single phonic rule. It is only necessary to teach the ones that occur most frequently in words that children will read and write. The following checklist is an important tool for teachers in kindergarten through second grade, where phonics is an important part of the total reading–writing curriculum. Teachers of older, struggling readers may also find it helpful. Effective teachers of systematic and explicit phonics

- Involve preschool, kindergarten, and children who are new to learning to read and write in activities that promote recognizing, naming, and associating letters with sounds.
- Include a comprehensive range of letter–sound patterns presented in a logical and systematic sequence.
- Begin by teaching simple, most common, and most useful letter–sound relationships and move to more complex patterns.
- Help children use analogies to decode and spell new words.
- Assess and evaluate children's development regularly.
- Group children for instruction based on their needs and level of phonic understanding.
- Make sure that students can apply their understandings of phonics generalizations in their reading and writing.

Suggested Reading on Phonics

Bear, D. R., Invernizzi, M., Templeton, S., & Johnston, F. (2004). *Words their way: Word study for phonics, vocabulary, and spelling instruction.* Upper Saddle River, NJ: Pearson.

Cunningham, P. M. (2000). *Phonics they use: Words for reading and writing.* New York: Addison Wesley Longman.

Fluency

Fluency is defined by the NRP (2000) as "the ability to read with speed, accuracy, and proper expression" (p. 3-5), as opposed to word-by-word reading. Many researchers have noted that fluency is one of the most neglected aspects of literacy instruction (Allington, 1983; Reutzel & Hollingsworth, 1993; Samuels, 2002). It is clear that fluency plays an important role in overall reading development and is related to comprehension in three ways. First, readers must be able to identify words with sufficient speed so that cognitive resources are available to understand what is being read. The reader must be able to recognize words automatically, with little attention to decoding the words so that they can pay attention to the meaning of the text. Second, readers must read accurately so that they understand the message in the text. Readers are far less likely to understand the message if they can't identify the words on the page or if they simply guess. Finally, readers must be able to group words into phrases that are comprehensible. Oral language is naturally grouped into phrases that make it easier to comprehend. Written language relies on similar phrasing and punctuation to allow the reader to pause and make sense of the text. For these reasons, we'll define fluency as a factor of four items; speed, accuracy, expression, and comprehension.

What Research Says about Fluency

Fluent readers decode text automatically and can devote their attention to comprehending what is read (LaBerge & Samuels, 1974). If a child's reading is slow and labored, the child cannot remember what he or she reads. Carnine, Silbert, and Kame'enui (1997) found that less-fluent readers have poorer comprehension. Rasinski, Pakak, and Dallinga (1991) found that a majority of struggling readers had difficulties in reading fluency. The NRP (2000) found that

- Fluency develops over time and through ample practice reading.
- Guided oral reading with feedback is one of the most effective strategies for developing fluency.
- Repeated and monitored oral reading improves fluency.
- Attention to fluency improves word recognition and comprehension.
- Attention to fluency is appropriate for all age ranges, especially struggling readers.
- Through practice, children can improve their overall reading fluency.

Fluency in the Classroom

The consensus from researchers is that guided repeated oral reading with feedback is one of the most effective strategies for developing fluency (NRP, 2000). This involves having children read and reread the same text three to five times with assistance from a teacher, parents, classmates, or reading tutors. This can be accomplished through children reading a book chorally, shared reading of big books or chart dictated stories, or paired reading with more-fluent readers. Guided repeated oral reading helps children improve their abilities to read difficult words, phrase text with confidence, and comprehend text.

Feedback is a critical element in the development of fluency in all of these approaches. This happens when the teacher or more-capable reader provides information about the reader's performance. For example, the teacher may comment on how the child's voice rises with excitement while reading, how the child uses punctuation to phrase his or her reading, or how the child set an appropriate pace.

Although there are many approaches that will develop fluency, children benefit from listening to examples of fluent reading. Teachers, parents, classmates, and reading tutors should read text aloud to children so that they can hear fluent, expressive reading in a variety of genres. Not only will this promote fluency by allowing children to hear the rhythm and structure of various forms of text, but it also increases their vocabularies by exposing them to the words authors use in books. Additionally, it helps build a long-term love of reading.

Johns and Berglund (2002) state that the following evidence-based strategies also improve fluency:

- *Basic sight words* are the most common words that occur over and over in the English language. These words can comprise over 60 percent of the words used in beginning reading materials and over 50 percent of the words used in materials used in the upper grades.

- *Language experience approach* (LEA) involves writing down what children say, then reading and rereading it with them to develop knowledge of letter–sound associations, sight words, prosody, and language.

- *Readers theater* is a presentation of a text read aloud expressively and dramatically by two or more readers.

- *Echo reading* involves the child immediately echoing or imitating the performance of a more skilled reader.

- *Choral reading* involves children reading text in unison.

- *Phrase boundaries* involve clustering reading into appropriate phrases, rather than reading word by word.

- *Paired reading* involves a more capable reader supporting a tutee in reading materials that are generally more difficult than those read independently.

- *Neurological impress method* involves the teacher and the child reading aloud simultaneously from the same book. The teacher reads slightly faster than the child to keep the reading fluent. The teacher usually sits next to the child and focuses his or her voice near the ear of the child while pointing to the words as they are read.

- *Repeated reading* involves children reading text while the teacher rates the children's speed and accuracy. The child practices reading the passage orally or silently several times. After practicing, the teacher listens to the child read and again rates the speed and accuracy. The teacher and child compare before and after results and graph growth using a chart.

- *Computer-based or tape-assisted reading* involves using computer or tape-recorded text to assist and model reading for students.

A Note on Round-Robin Reading

Many teachers will confuse guided oral reading with round-robin reading. They are *not* the same. Round-robin reading involves one child reading text aloud while a group of children listen (and presumably follow along), waiting for their turn to read aloud. There is no evidence that round-robin reading promotes fluency. In fact,

Opitz and Rasinski (1998) claim that it is an outdated instructional method that may actually cause reading problems. They claim that there is often no time for children to rehearse before reading aloud and this may cause undue stress, anxiety, and embarrassment for the struggling reader who must perform in front of his or her classmates. It slows down the reading speed of those who follow along, promoting boredom, inattention, and misbehavior. Most importantly, it wastes valuable classroom time. Opitz and Rasinski suggest alternatives to round-robin reading, including independent reading, buddy or partner reading, listening to the teacher read aloud, listening to a classmate read aloud, and computer- or tape-assisted reading.

The ability to read any text with fluency depends on several factors. First, the child must read a text that is at his or her instructional level. This means that the vast majority of the words in the text must be known (generally 90 percent or more) so that little attention is given to decoding words. If a child is reading a text that requires him or her to stop and decode too many words, then fluency rates will decline. Second, the child must have some background or interest in reading the text. If a child finds the text interesting or has some knowledge about the subject, he or she is more likely to be fluent when reading the text. Some children may be more fluent on texts about motorcycles or insects because they have an interest in those topics and are more familiar with the words and concepts associated with the topic. Finally, fluency will vary depending on the child's familiarity with the text. The first time a child reads a text, he or she will naturally be less fluent than the third or fourth time. For this reason, repeated reading of text is a powerful tool to increase fluency. A child can notice and celebrate his or her increased fluency on a text after successive readings. The biggest benefit from using these methods comes from modeling, feedback, and repetition.

With those factors in mind, it is important to have a large repertoire of texts in the classroom. Teachers should have a well-stocked classroom library of different genres from a variety of reading levels so that all children in their classrooms can find books that are of interest to them at their reading level. The core reading program or basal reader must contain text that is at an appropriate level as well. Children who are struggling with grade-level text will need easier text, perhaps from the previous grade. Children reading above grade level will need texts that go beyond what the grade-level basal provides.

Commercial programs, such as *QuickReads* from Modern Curriculum Press, have also proven to be successful and promote fluency. Most commercial programs consist of a wide variety of texts from different genres and reading levels, teacher resource manuals that describe how to implement the program, audio tapes or CDs that model fluent reading for children, and some include interactive computer programs that use speech-recognition technology. For all commercial programs, teachers are encouraged to review the research studies done on the program and carefully review the program to determine if it meets the needs of the students in their schools and classrooms.

A Note on Sustained Silent Reading (SSR)

The NRP reached a startling conclusion when they stated that there was no evidence to support encouraging children to do more independent reading in school. There were surprisingly few studies included in the NRP's report, and many of those studies were short in duration with none lasting more than a year. The NRP stated that "while encouraging students to read [on their own] might be beneficial, research has not yet demonstrated this in a clear and convincing manner" (p. 3-3). Few educators would argue that reading improves with practice. The more children read the more literate they become, although research has not yet demonstrated this compellingly.

We encourage all teachers, including kindergarten teachers, to set aside time for independent reading and for teachers to model the love of reading by reading themselves during sustained silent reading (SSR) or drop everything and read (DEAR). This means that children should have access to a wide variety of reading materials from well-stocked classroom libraries with a broad range of reading levels. Even the youngest readers benefit by engaging in independent reading. However, teachers can make their SSR or DEAR time more productive by making sure that children actually read during independent reading time, that there is time for children to discuss their reading, and by modeling how to select books that are at a child's reading level.

Fluency Checklist

"Fluency develops as a result of having multiple opportunities to practice reading skills with a high rate of success" (Honig, Diamond, & Gutlohn, 2000, p. 11). In order to accomplish this, teachers must provide children with opportunities to read texts that are not frustrating. The research findings suggest that rereading texts with feedback from a more-capable reader enhances fluency. The following checklist is provided to assist all teachers in evaluating fluency instruction in their classroom. In order to promote fluency, all teachers should

- Engage children in reading and rereading of texts at their instructional level (90 percent or greater accuracy).
- Model fluent reading by reading aloud from a variety of different genres.
- Assess reading rate, accuracy, and expression regularly.
- Provide children with feedback about their oral reading.
- *Not* use round-robin reading.

Suggested Reading on Fluency

Allington, R. L. (1983). Fluency: The neglected reading goal in reading instruction. *The Reading Teacher, 36,* 556–561.
Johns, J. L., & Berglund, R. L. (2002). *Fluency: Questions, answers, and evidence-based strategies.* Dubuque, IA: Kendall/Hunt.

Vocabulary

Simply stated, vocabulary is the words you know. Vocabulary instruction focuses on how children learn the meanings of new words and understand new meanings and concepts. Words are the foundation of reading. In order to understand any text, readers must not only be able to recall the meanings of words quickly and accurately, but also put meanings to words based on context and their own experiences. As you can see, vocabulary plays an important role in comprehension.

There are many types of vocabulary that play an essential role in learning to read. Oral vocabulary includes the words that readers are familiar with in speech. Readers, especially early and novice readers, link their knowledge of oral words to the words they read. They make connections between words they see in print (reading vocabulary) and the words they have in their oral vocabulary. If there is no match, then the reader will not understand the word. If an emergent reader lacks oral vocabulary, it is difficult for him or her to gain meaning from what is read.

What Research Says about Vocabulary

Although estimates vary, researchers suggest that students learn 3,000 to 5,000 words each year and have a core reading vocabulary of approximately 25,000 words by the end of elementary school (Anderson & Nagy, 1991; Nagy & Herman, 1987). It is also estimated that by fifth grade children may encounter more than a million words of written text a year (Nagy, Herman, & Anderson, 1985; Stahl, 1999). Children learn a majority of new words incidentally, without direct instruction (Kame'enui, Dixon, & Carnine, 1987). Vocabulary knowledge is related to children's text comprehension (Beck & McKeown, 1991). Preteaching the vocabulary of a new text does improve children's comprehension of that text and overall vocabulary development (Beck, Perfetti, & McKeown, 1982). Children who read more have larger vocabularies (Nagy & Anderson, 1984; Stanovich, 1986). The NRP found that

- Vocabulary instruction improves comprehension.
- Children learn a vast number of words through incidental learning.
- Wide reading promotes vocabulary development.
- Preteaching words improves vocabulary and comprehension.
- Repeated exposure to words improves vocabulary and comprehension.
- Vocabulary knowledge is significantly related to reading comprehension, decoding, spelling, and school achievement.

Vocabulary in the Classroom

Children come to school with vastly different funds of knowledge about words. They enter the classroom with different backgrounds, exposures to words and concepts, and cultural experiences. Teachers should capitalize on children's oral vocabularies, extend oral vocabulary, and broaden that knowledge into developing children's reading vocabulary. In preschool and the early elementary years, fostering word learning should be a high-priority goal, especially for children who might be at risk or are struggling to learn to read.

Teaching vocabulary is more than just teaching the meanings of words. Rather, it involves an in-depth knowledge of words. In addition to understanding word meanings, children need to be able to apply appropriate meanings based on context and background knowledge and experience, and be able to generalize meanings of words in new contexts. Vocabulary can be learned in a variety of ways, including independent reading, listening to books read aloud, direct instruction, and student-centered activities. Beck and McKeown (1991) suggest the following principles for effective vocabulary instruction across the curriculum:

- All approaches to teaching vocabulary are more effective than no instruction.
- No one approach has been shown to be consistently best.
- Multiple approaches and activities yield the best gains in vocabulary knowledge.
- Repeated exposures to vocabulary words increase understanding.

If we are to assume that children learn 3,000 to 5,000 words per year, it is obviously impossible to learn a sizable portion of these new words through direct instruction approaches. Nagy (1988) stresses, "the single most important thing a teacher can do to promote vocabulary growth is to increase students' volume of reading" (p. 38). Hayes and Ahrens (1988) found that speech is far more limited than written language in terms of exposure to new vocabulary. Typical day-to-day oral language experiences for children do not contain enough new or interesting words to bring about significant vocabulary growth. Therefore, a significant source of word knowledge is exposure to print through wide reading. Wide reading encompasses the volume of reading (number of words) and the different genres (types of texts).

Books introduce children to more new words than conversation or television (Snow, Burns, & Griffin, 1998). *Book language* is a more sophisticated vocabulary that children rarely hear in everyday language. An author may use the word *sauntered* for *walked* or the word *hypothesis* for *guess*. These types of words vary from author to author and genre to genre. Therefore, teachers should expose children to many different authors, fiction, nonfiction, poetry, and other forms of text.

In addition to providing opportunities for incidental word learning, teachers should take time to explicitly teach vocabulary. This involves directly teaching word meanings. Research indicates that preteaching vocabulary before children read has a significant effect on vocabulary development and comprehension. Before children read, teachers should read through the text and select vocabulary that might be unfamiliar. Even when vocabulary lists are provided (such as lists found with basal reading programs), teachers are encouraged to preteach only those words that may be challenging for the children in their classrooms. Beck and McKeown (1991) suggest that teachers carefully evaluate the words they preteach. Teachers may not be able to preteach all of the words that are unfamiliar to children so they should prioritize based on the following criteria:

- Is the word important to comprehending the text?
- Will children encounter this word again in the text or in other texts?
- Will knowing that word help in other areas of the curriculum?

Explicit instruction also involves emphasizing vocabulary after reading. Teachers should take advantage of class discussions to reinforce vocabulary and concepts children have learned after reading. Actively involving them in discussions allows children to make connections between the vocabulary they are learning and their own experiences. It also allows teachers opportunities to model word learning strategies and allows children to share their own effective strategies for figuring out unknown words. For example, teachers can model how to use context, how to use word parts (prefixes, suffixes, root words, etc.), and how to use the dictionary to determine word meaning. Repetition and multiple exposures to vocabulary in different contexts can have significant effects on children's word learning.

A Note on the Use of Dictionaries

Many of us remember vocabulary as endless lists of words for which we had to copy definitions from the dictionary and write sentences. Miller and Gildea (1987) examined the errors children made when writing sentences based on dictionary definitions and concluded that this practice was "pedagogically useless" (p. 98). They state that although the dictionary can be a powerful tool to develop word knowledge, it seems that instruction that focuses on looking up words and writing sentences produces superficial understandings of words and leads to rapid forgetting of words.

Moreover, there are other considerations for young children when using the dictionary. Many children find it difficult to locate words in dictionaries. The sheer number of words in dictionaries and lack of alphabetic knowledge may quickly lead to frustration. Dictionaries routinely oversimplify definitions due to space limitations. Definitions often lack rich explanations of words and few dictionaries provide meanings of words based on the exact context from which children encounter new words. For this reason, it may be difficult to find a suitable definition.

Even with all of these limitations, the dictionary can be a useful tool if teachers model the flexible thinking involved in using a dictionary to figure out what new words mean. The sophisticated process must include modeling and thinking aloud about how to find a word, how to select an appropriate definition, using context to confirm and extend the meaning, and how to apply the newly acquired word knowledge to different contexts. This complicated process is usually beyond what many young readers can do independently and is unlikely to promote vocabulary development if students are solely responsible for orchestrating all of these complex aspects.

New words should be introduced before reading and reinforced after reading using both their definitions and the context in which they are used. The NRP (2000) found that combining both definition and context enhances children's vocabulary development and comprehension. Teachers can reword or rephrase definitions to help children learn word meanings as well as synonyms and antonyms. Using examples and nonexamples helps children develop a clearer understanding of concepts. Context will also change a word's meaning from one situation to another. Graphic organizers are ways to visually show connections between new vocabulary and concepts behind the words.

Teachers should explicitly teach word-learning strategies. The most common and successful strategies seem to be context clues, using word parts (prefixes, root words, syllables, etc.), graphic organizers, and using the dictionary (Graves & Watts-Taffe, 2002). Teachers can model these strategies for children through *thinking aloud* and describing the processes they use to unlock the meanings of unfamiliar words. For example, when reading a text aloud to children, teachers can talk about how they derive meanings of words based on the surrounding words and sentences in the text.

Children learn as many words while listening to text read aloud as they do by reading themselves (Stahl, Richek, & Vandevier, 1991). Reading aloud exposes children to the more formal *book language* that they might not be exposed to through day-to-day oral language experiences. Because many struggling readers are reluctant to read themselves, reading aloud to them is one of the most powerful ways to increase their exposure to the more formal vocabulary found in books.

Teachers need to help children develop word consciousness. Graves and Watts-Taffe (2002) define word consciousness as the "awareness of and interest in words and their meanings" (p. 142). Children who have word consciousness are aware of the words around them, understand how words enhance their understandings, and are motivated to seek out new and interesting words. Teachers can help foster this by pointing out interesting words and phrases and by encouraging children to find their own examples in the books they listen to and read. For example, as teachers read stories aloud to children, they might write interesting words or phrases on charts and encourage students to *borrow* these words and phrases in their own speaking and writing.

The International Reading Association's summary of the NRP report (International Reading Association, n.d.) points out that the NRP was reluctant to identify any single method that was more effective. Instead, they note that using a variety of methods seems to be most effective. The methods include keyword method (children learn new words by learning a keyword clue for each vocabulary word), incidental learning (most vocabulary is learned through reading or listening to others read), repeated exposure (using new vocabulary across the curriculum), preteaching of vocabulary, restructuring reading materials (such as substituting an easier synonym for a harder word), and context method (children use clues in the text to figure out new words).

Vocabulary Checklist

Children learn an astonishing number of words every year. They learn new vocabulary in classrooms where they have opportunities to learn words that are explicitly taught and they learn through reading and listening to books read aloud. Classrooms that promote vocabulary development include ample opportunities for children to

- Listen to texts read aloud from many different genres.
- Engage in independent, wide reading.
- Learn words from explicit instruction in word meanings and concepts.
- Talk about words before, during, and after reading.
- Explicitly teach and model word-learning strategies.
- Use vocabulary that they have learned in their speaking and writing.
- Experience multiple exposures to words.
- Develop their own word consciousness.

Suggested Reading on Vocabulary

Beck, I., McKeown, M. G., & Kucan, L. (2002). *Bringing words to life: Robust vocabulary instruction.* New York: Guilford.
Stahl, S. A. (1999). *Vocabulary development.* Cambridge, MA: Brookline Books.

Comprehension

The NRP (2000) quotes Durkin (1993), stating that comprehension has come to be viewed as "the essence of reading" (p. 4). Comprehension is more than just answering questions to determine what children know after reading text. The goal of reading is comprehension—negotiating and constructing meaning from written text. Comprehension occurs when readers consciously apply strategies or procedures to understand text. It is important to note that comprehension is a process, not an event. Readers don't just understand text after they have finished reading it. Instead, they negotiate meaning before, during, and after they read. As quoted in *The Literacy Dictionary* (Harris & Hodges, 1995), Ruddell, Ruddell, and Singer (1994) state:

> Comprehension is a process in which the reader constructs meaning [in] interacting with text . . . through a combination of prior knowledge and previous experience; information available in text; the stance [taken] in relationship to the text; and immediate, remembered or anticipated social interactions and communications. (p. 39)

Comprehension strategies are plans or procedures beyond those skills that are automatic that readers use and apply when they read or listen to text read aloud. Examples of comprehension strategies include predicting, self-monitoring, identifying the main idea, and summarizing.

What Research Says about Comprehension

If children cannot decode words in text, they will not understand what they read (Adams, 1990). Fluency influences reading comprehension because children who cannot decode words quickly and accurately do not understand what they read (LaBerge & Samuels, 1974). Vocabulary instruction improves children's vocabulary and reading comprehension (Beck & McKeown, 1991; Beck, Perfetti, & McKeown, 1982; Stanovich, 1986, 1994). Children can be directly taught comprehension strategies and they transfer the use of them in their independent reading (Block & Pressley, 2002; Duffy, 1993; Pressley, 2002; Pressley, Johnson, Symons, McGoldrick, & Kurita, 1989). Background knowledge influences comprehension (Hansen & Pearson, 1983; Spires, Gallini, & Riggsbee, 1992; Tharp, 1982). Studies of exemplary primary-grade teachers document that they attend to comprehension as well as word identification and decoding skills (Morrow, Tracey, Woo, & Pressley, 1999; Taylor, Pearson, Clark, & Walpole, 1999). Attending to word identification and decoding is not sufficient to promote comprehension development (Adams, 1990). The NRP (2000) concluded that

- Explicit comprehension strategy instruction improves children's reading comprehension.
- Teaching a variety of reading comprehension strategies in natural settings and content areas improves comprehension.
- Explicit instruction and modeling have been successful in improving comprehension and improvement on standardized tests.

Comprehension in the Classroom

Effective comprehension instruction should begin with an understanding of what capable readers do when they read and comprehend text. According to Duke and Pearson (2002), researchers have documented a great deal about this. They describe these characteristics by stating that good readers

- Are active when they read
- Have clear goals in mind when reading and evaluate as they read to determine if the text is meeting their goals
- Preview the text before they read
- Make predictions throughout their reading
- Read selectively, making decisions about what to read quickly, what not to read, what to reread, etc.
- Construct, revise, and question the meaning they make as they read
- Try to determine the meanings of unfamiliar words
- Draw from their own experiences and integrate their experiences with the material in the text
- Monitor their understanding and make adjustments to their reading as necessary
- Read different kinds of texts differently
- Attend to setting and characters when reading narrative text
- Construct and revise summaries of what they have read when reading expository text

If teachers understand what capable readers do to comprehend text, the next logical question is can we teach children these same qualities? The answer, according to Duke and Pearson (2002), is a resounding yes! Research indicates that teachers can help children learn the strategies they need in order to comprehend a wide variety of texts.

A Note on Decoding and Comprehension

It stands to reason that if children have poor decoding skills they will be poor at comprehending text. If children cannot identify the words on the page, how can they understand the written text? The short answer is they cannot. Therefore, careful attention to word identification and decoding skills is critical for beginning readers.

However, focusing on word identification and decoding alone are not sufficient to promote good readers who comprehend what they read in the primary grades. Many teachers in the primary grades emphasize word recognition and decoding with little attention to comprehension strategies. Unfortunately, it seems that waiting for comprehension instruction until the intermediate grades is too late. Pearson and Duke (2002) state "to delay this sort of powerful instruction until children have reached the intermediate grades is to deny them the very experiences that help them develop the most important of reading dispositions—the expectation that they should and can understand each and every text they read" (p. 257).

Teachers must emphasize effective comprehension instruction throughout schooling, including all of the elementary years, middle/junior high years, and through high school years and beyond.

Analysis of the NRP (2000) report indicated that the NRP found several general strategies to be highly effective in improving children's comprehension.

- *Comprehension monitoring* involves children learning to be aware of their understanding of the text and to use specific fix-up strategies when needed. Comprehension monitoring is a form of metacognition, or thinking about thinking. Children ask themselves, "Is what I'm reading making sense?" and "What can I do to make sure I understand what I'm reading?"

- *Cooperative learning* has children working together to learn and discuss comprehension strategies. This leads to children taking more control over their learning and increases interactions with peers.

- *Graphic organizers* are visuals that allow children to organize ideas and concepts. They help children understand how ideas are interrelated and facilitate the recall of information. Venn diagrams, story maps, T-charts, KWL charts, and webbing are all types of graphic organizers.

- *Story structure* is the elements that make up stories, including plot, characters, setting, point of view, and theme. As children read, they ask and answer who, what, when, where, why, and how questions. They can also map time lines, characters, and story events.

- *Question answering* involves teachers posing questions and guiding children to the correct answers, enabling them to learn more from the text.

- *Question generating* has children asking themselves and their peers what, where, when, why, what will happen, how, and who questions.

- *Summarization* involves children identifying and verbalizing or writing the main ideas from their reading.

Although each of these strategies was effective alone, the NRP also found that combining multiple strategies was also very effective. A teacher models a blended approach by showing how she or he would try to understand the text using a combination of two or more strategies. For example, a teacher might model how to use a graphic organizer to identify and show relationships between story elements.

How do teachers go about teaching these strategies? Duffy (2002) suggests that direct explanation of strategies is the best way to help readers, especially struggling readers, understand and use comprehension strategies. In order to accomplish this, teachers must model and discuss the strategies they use as they read. This helps children learn

- What the strategy is and why it is important
- How, when, and where to use the strategy

- Which strategies work best in certain texts
- How to apply different strategies to different texts and reading situations

Teachers are encouraged to follow modeling with guided practice and appropriate feedback. In the beginning considerable support is needed. However, over time that support is gradually reduced as children become more successful in applying strategies on their own. Pearson and Gallagher (1983) state that gradual release of control from the teacher to the child encourages children and empowers them to self-regulate the use of the strategy.

It is recommended that teachers begin by teaching one strategy at a time. Children should practice the strategy in a variety of texts. Devote ample time for children to take control over the strategy before introducing a new strategy. Finally, directly teach and model how two strategies can be used together.

What does it look like for a good reader when all of the strategies are pulled together? Figure 3.2 represents some of the elements that good readers employ during the entire reading process. Skilled readers select the strategies that work best for them and seem appropriate for the text they are reading. Therefore, not every element will be used in every text. Similarly, the elements will not be used in the same order for every reading experience. The figure is provided to give an overall understanding of the complex strategies good readers use in order to comprehend text.

Although providing quality, explicit instruction in comprehension strategies is highly effective, it is not enough. Just as with phonics, explicit instruction in comprehension will only be effective if children have many opportunities to apply their new skills and strategies in reading lots of books. Children must become flexible in their application of the strategies in many different types of text. The success of these strategies also depends on the quality and variety of materials children read. The classroom environment should be rich in discussions about text (both teacher–child and child–child) so that children benefit from being able to relate the text to their own experiences and benefit from listening to their peers' experiences and application of strategies.

It is never too early to emphasize comprehension instruction. Even before children can read independently they benefit from listening to, responding to, and analyzing text that is read to them. Teachers can model the same comprehension strategies while reading text aloud to children, familiarizing them with the strategies and preparing them to use those strategies when they begin reading text.

Comprehension Checklist

Comprehension instruction in the primary grades is not only possible but beneficial to overall reading development (Pearson & Duke, 2002). In order to promote the use of comprehension strategies, teachers should

- Establish solid decoding and word identification skills.
- Emphasize fluency and vocabulary.
- Provide a wide variety of texts for children to read.

FIGURE 3.2   **Strategies Used by Good Readers before, during, and after Reading**

Before Reading

- Activate and use prior knowledge.
- Make connections between content of the text and real-life experiences.
- Set a purpose for reading.
- Determine what strategies might be used with the text.
- Use graphic organizers.
- Visualize or develop mental images.
- Predict what the text might be about.

During Reading

- Monitor comprehension.
- Continue making and revising predictions.
- Identify the main idea.
- Summarize.
- Answer and generate questions.
- Stop periodically to get the gist of the text.
- Apply fix-up strategies when the text doesn't make sense.
- Determine appropriate strategies for reading the text.
- Visualize or develop mental images.
- Make inferences.

After Reading

- Answer and generate questions.
- Identify the main idea.
- Summarize.
- Discuss.
- Share information.
- Determine what information is important to know and remember.
- Use graphic organizers to organize important information and show connections.
- Visualize or develop mental images.

- Create a classroom environment where children participate in discussions about the texts they read.
- Explicitly teach strategies when children read text.
- Model strategies when reading aloud to children.
- Provide lots of practice opportunities for children to independently use comprehension strategies in reading books.
- Monitor progress through informal reading inventories, retelling, and participation in discussions.

Suggested Reading on Comprehension

Duke, N. K., & Bennett-Armistead, S. V. (2003). *Reading and writing informational texts in the primary grades: Research-based practices.* New York: Scholastic.

Block, C. C., & Pressley, M. (Eds.). (2002). *Comprehension instruction: Research-based best practices.* New York: Guilford Press.

How Are the Essential Elements Incorporated into a Core Reading Program?

One of the major elements of the Reading First legislation is to ensure that states, districts, and schools establish reading programs for students in kindergarten through third grade that are based on scientific reading research and that every child can read at grade level or above no later than the end of third grade. Funding for the adoption of core reading programs is included in state and local grants that allow schools to adopt high-quality reading programs that have proven track records for teaching children to read and addressing all of the essential elements of reading. Although there is no one single program that will teach all children to read, comprehensive reading programs should include a collection of instructional practices that have been tested and have a proven record of success. Comprehensive reading programs are the primary instructional tool used by teachers to teach reading. Programs should include:

- Research-based instructional strategies that explicitly teach strategies and skills
- Systematic and sequential instruction that moves children from simple to more complex skills and strategies
- Ample practice opportunities that allow children to practice skills and strategies in reading and writing text
- A ninety-minute or more uninterrupted block of time for reading instruction per day
- Assessment tools for diagnosing children's needs and monitoring progress
- Professional development that will ensure teachers have the skills necessary to implement the program effectively and meet the needs of their children

The biggest challenge is determining if a program is a good match for the children and teachers at an individual school. The first step in choosing a core reading program should be to complete an assessment of the school's needs. The following guidelines (International Reading Association, 2002; North Central Regional Laboratory, n.d.) provide schools with the necessary information to make informed decisions about what programs to adopt at their site.

Guidelines for Adopting Scientifically Based Reading Researched Core Reading Programs

1. What are the needs of the children at your school?
   Does the school have English language learners?
   Does the school have a minority population?
   Does the school have a migrant population?
   Does the school have a population of exceptional children?
   What are the reading strengths of the children at your school?
   What are the reading weaknesses of the children at your school?
   What are the needs of the exceptional children?

How can the staff use present assessment procedures to assess students?
What additional assessments will be needed to plan for instruction?

2. What research supports the program?

What research has been done on the program?
Is the research published in a peer-reviewed journal or approved by a panel of independent, expert reviewers?
Is the research based on tests of the program itself or on similar strategies used under other circumstances?
Is the data valid and reliable? Will the data remain the same if collected at different locations with similar characteristics?
What are the outcomes for different subgroups (socioeconomic, race, gender, etc.)?
What was the duration of the program before measurable progress was made?

3. What is the cost of the program?

What additional resources will have to be purchased to implement the program (workbooks, literature, etc.)?
Are additional personnel needed to implement the program?
How can existing resources support the program?

4. How difficult is the implementation of this program?

How complex is the program?
How comfortable are the teachers with the program?
Has the program been used by schools in the surrounding area and what are the results?
Will teachers' current levels of knowledge about scientifically based reading research adequately prepare them to use the program?

5. What professional development will be needed to implement the program?

Is additional training necessary to implement the program?
Will training be ongoing and sustained throughout the school year?
What is needed to sustain the program through changes in personnel?

Many states have established criteria for selecting core reading programs. Districts, schools, and teachers should use this information to evaluate whether reading programs meet the criteria for addressing scientifically based reading research as well as meet the needs of the teachers and children in individual schools. A review of these programs requires an in-depth and critical analysis. Simmons and Kame'enui (2003) offer *A Consumer's Guide to Evaluating a Core Reading Program Grades K–3: A Critical Elements Analysis,* a set of guidelines for reviewing reading programs grade by grade. Their guidelines begin with an examination of the scientific evidence of the program's effectiveness and move to a critical analysis of the program's ability to meet all of the state's standards, including the essential components as outlined in the NRP (2000) report. Each grade level has an extensive checklist to determine what high-priority and discretionary elements are included in the program. You can download a copy at http://reading.uoregon.edu/appendices/con_guide_3.1.03.pdf.

Many schools have already adopted a core reading program before making a critical analysis to determine if it meets these criteria. An analysis of this program is still very important. It will help teachers and administrators determine what scientifically based reading elements or practices are already in place. The school can also determine what resources, instructional practices, professional development, and materials will need to be added. The final step should be integrating all of these elements into one comprehensive curriculum.

Conclusion

We began this chapter by stating that the legislation behind Reading First placed a heavy emphasis on the use of scientifically based reading research on the five essential elements of reading. Teachers are expected to know and use this information in order to provide high-quality reading instruction so that all children can learn to read. Based on the contents of this chapter, what would a Reading First classroom look like?

1. The teacher understands the scientifically based reading research and can identify reading practices that have been tested and proven effective with children.
2. The teacher applies scientifically based reading research through explicit and systematic instruction in all of the essential reading components:
   - Phonemic awareness
   - Phonics
   - Fluency
   - Vocabulary
   - Comprehension
3. The teacher provides ample opportunities for children to use explicitly and systematically taught skills and strategies in the reading and writing of texts.
4. The teacher uses a core reading program that has proven to be effective and includes all of the essential components.

References

Adams, M. J. (1990). *Beginning to read: Thinking and learning about print.* Cambridge, MA: MIT Press.

Adams, M. J., Foorman, B. R., Lundberg, I., & Beeler, T. (1998). *Phonemic awareness in young children: A classroom curriculum.* Baltimore: Paul H. Brooks.

Allington, R. L. (1983). Fluency: The neglected reading goal in reading instruction. *The Reading Teacher, 36,* 556–561.

Allington, R. L., & Woodside-Jiron, H. (1998). Decodable text in beginning reading: Are mandates and policy based on research? *ERS Spectrum, 16,* 3–11.

Anderson, R. C., & Nagy, W. E. (1991). Word meaning. In R. Barr, M. L. Kamil, P. B. Mosenthal, & P. D. Pearson (Eds.), *Handbook of reading research* (Vol. 2) (pp. 690–724). White Plains, NY: Longman.

Ball, E. W., & Blachman, B. A. (1991). Does phonemic awareness training in kindergarten make a difference in early word recognition and developmental spelling? *Reading Research Quarterly, 26,* 49–66.

Bear, D. R., Invernizzi, M., Templeton, S., & Johnston, F. (2004). *Words their way: Word study for phonics, vocabulary, and spelling instruction.* Upper Saddle River, NJ: Pearson.

Beck, I. (1997). Response to "overselling phonics." *Reading Today, 15,* 17.

Beck, I., & McKeown, M. (1991). Conditions of vocabulary acquisition. In R. Barr, M. L. Kamil, P. Mosenthal, & P. D. Pearson (Eds.), *Handbook of reading research* (Vol. 2) (pp. 789–814). White Plains, NY: Longman.

Beck, I., McKeown, M. G., & Kucan, L. (2002). *Bringing words to life: Robust vocabulary instruction.* New York: Guilford.

Beck, I. L., Perfetti, C. A., & McKeown, M. G. (1982). The effects of long-term vocabulary instruction on lexical access and reading comprehension. *Journal of Educational Psychology, 74,* 506–521.

Blachman, B. A., Ball, E. W., Black, R., & Tangle, D. M. (2000). *Road to the code: A phonological awareness program for young children.* Baltimore: Paul H. Brooks.

Block, C. C., & Pressley, M. (Eds.). (2002). *Comprehension instruction: Research-based best practices.* New York: Guilford.

Carnine, D. W., Silbert, J., & Kame'enui, E. J. (1997). *Direct instruction reading.* Upper Saddle River, NJ: Prentice-Hall.

Chall, J. S. (1967). *Learning to read: The great debate.* New York: McGraw-Hill.

Cunningham, P. M. (2000). *Phonics they use: Words for reading and writing.* New York: Addison Wesley Longman.

Duffy, G. (1993). Re-thinking strategy instruction: Teacher development and low achievers' understandings. *Elementary School Journal, 93,* 231–247.

Duffy, G. (2002). The case for direct explanation of strategies. In C. C. Block & M. Pressley (Eds.), *Comprehension instruction: Research-based best practices* (pp. 28–41). New York: Guildford.

Duke, N. K., & Bennett-Armistead, S. V. (2003). *Reading and writing informational texts in the primary grades: Research-based practices.* New York: Scholastic.

Duke, N., & Pearson, P. D. (2002). Effective practices for developing reading comprehension. In A. E. Farstrup & S. J. Samuels (Eds.), *What research has to say about reading instruction* (pp. 205–242). Newark, DE: International Reading Association.

Durkin, D. (1993). *Teaching them to read.* Boston: Allyn and Bacon.

Farstrup, A. E., & Samuels, S. J. (Eds.). (2002). *What research has to say about reading instruction* (3rd ed.). Newark, DE: International Reading Association.

Graves, M. F., & Watts-Taffe, S. M. (2002). The place of word consciousness in a research-based vocabulary program. In A. E. Farstrup & S. J. Samuels (Eds.), *What research has to say about reading instruction* (pp. 140–165). Newark, DE: International Reading Association.

Griffith, P. L., & Olson, M. W. (1992). Phonemic awareness helps beginning readers break the code. *The Reading Teacher, 45,* 516–523.

Hall, S. L., & Moats, L. C. (1999). *Straight talk about reading: How parents can make a difference during the early years.* Lincolnwood, IL: NTC/Contemporary Publishing Group.

Hansen, J., & Pearson, P. D. (1983). An instructional study: Improving the inferential comprehending instruction on the comprehension of good and poor fourth grade readers. *Journal of Educational Psychology, 75,* 821–829.

Harris, T. L., & Hodges, R. E. (1995). *The literacy dictionary: The vocabulary of reading and writing.* Newark, DE: International Reading Association.

Hayes D. P., & Ahrens, M. G. (1998). Vocabulary simplification for children: A special case of "motherease"? *Journal of Child Language, 15,* 2.

Hiebert, E. H. (1999). Text matters in learning to read. *Reading Teacher, 52,* 552–566.

Honig, B., Diamond, L., & Gutlohn, L. (2000). *Teaching reading sourcebook for kindergarten through eighth grade.* Novato, CA: Arena Press.

International Reading Association (IRA). (2002). What is evidence-based reading instruction? A position statement of the International Reading Association. Retrieved February 15, 2004, from http://www.reading.org/pdf/1055.pdf.

International Reading Association (IRA). (n.d.). *International Reading Association's Summary of the (U.S.) National Reading Panel Report "Teaching Children to Read."* Retrieved February 1, 2004, from http://www.reading.org/advocacy/nrp/index.html.

Jenkins, J. R., Vadasy, P. F., Peyton, J. A., & Sanders, E. A. (2003). Decodable text: Where to find it. *The Reading Teacher, 57,* 185–189.

Johns, J. L., & Berglund, R. L. (2002). *Fluency: Questions, answers, and evidence-based strategies.* Dubuque, IA: Kendall/Hunt.

Juel, C., Griffith, P., & Gough, P. (1986). Acquisition of literacy: A longitudinal study of children in first and second grade. *Journal of Educational Psychology, 78,* 243–255.

Kame'enui, E. J., Dixon, D. W., & Carnine, D. (1987). Issues in the design of vocabulary instruction. In M. G. McKeown & M. E. Curtis (Eds.), *The nature of vocabulary acquisition* (pp. 129–145). Mahwah, NJ: Erlbaum.

Kame'enui, E. J., & Simmons, D. (1997). Decodable texts and the language of dichotomy: A response to Allington. *Reading Today, 15,* 18.

LaBerge, D., & Samuels, S. J. (1974). Toward a theory of automatic information processing in reading. *Cognitive Psychology, 6,* 293–323.

Miller, G., & Gildea, P. (1987). How children learn words. *Scientific American, 257,* 94–99.

Morrow, L. M., Tracey, D. H., Woo, D. G., & Pressley, G. M. (1999). Characteristics of exemplary first-grade literacy instruction. *The Reading Teacher, 52,* 462–476.

Nagy, W. E. (1988). *Vocabulary instruction and reading comprehension* (Technical report No. 431). Champaign, IL: Center for the Study of Reading.

Nagy, W. E., & Anderson, R. C. (1984). How many words are there in printed school English? *Reading Research Quarterly, 19,* 304–330.

Nagy, W. E., & Herman, P. A. (1987). Breadth and depth of vocabulary knowledge: Implications for acquisition and instruction. In M. G. McKeown & E. Curtis (Eds.), *The nature of vocabulary acquisition* (pp. 19–35). Mahwah, NJ: Erlbaum.

Nagy, W. E., Herman, P. A., & Anderson, R. C. (1985). Learning words from context. *Reading Research Quarterly, 20,* 233–253.

National Institute for Literacy. (2001). *Reading: Know what works.* Washington, DC: Office of Elementary and Secondary Education, Title I Programs.

National Reading Panel (NRP). (2000). *Teaching children to read: An evidence-based assessment of the scientific research literature on reading and its implications for reading instruction.* Washington, DC: National Institute of Child Health and Human Development.

North Central Regional Laboratory. (n.d.). Resources and information for state education agencies with Reading First grants. Retrieved February 1, 2004, from http://www.ncrel.org/rf.

Opitz, M. F., & Rasinski, T. V. (1998). Good-bye round robin: 25 effective oral reading strategies. Portsmouth, NH: Heinemann.

Pearson, P. D., & Duke, N. K. (2002). Comprehension instruction in the primary grades. In C. C. Block & M. Pressley (Eds.), *Comprehension instruction: Research-based best practices* (pp. 247–258). New York: Guilford.

Pearson, P. D., & Gallagher, M. (1983). The instruction of reading comprehension. *Contemporary Educational Psychology, 8,* 317–344.

Pressley, M. (2002). Comprehension strategies instruction: A turn-of-the-century status report. In C. C. Block & M. Pressley (Eds.), *Comprehension instruction: Research-based best practices* (pp. 11–27). New York: Guilford.

Pressley, M., Johnson, C. J., Symons, S., McGoldrick, J. S., & Kurita, J. A. (1989). Strategies that improve children's memory and comprehension of text. *Elementary School Journal, 90,* 3–32.

Rasinski, T. V., Pakak, N. D., & Dallinga, G. (1991). *Incidences of difficulty in reading fluency.* Paper presented at the annual meeting of the College Reading Association, Crystal City, VA.

Reutzel, D. R., & Hollingsworth, P. M. (1993). Effects of fluency training on second graders' reading comprehension. *Journal of Educational Research, 83,* 325–331.

Ruddell, R. M., Ruddell, M. P., & Singer, H. (Eds.). (1994). *Theoretical models and processes of reading*

(4th ed.). Newark, DE: International Reading Association.

Samuels, S. J. (2002). Reading fluency: Its development and assessment. In A. E. Farstrup & S. J. Samuels (Eds.), *What research has to say about reading instruction.* Newark, DE: International Reading Association.

Simmons, D. C., & Kame'enui, E. J. (2003). *A consumer's guide to evaluating a core reading program grades K–3: A critical elements analysis.* Retrieved February 15, 2004, from http://reading.uoregon.edu/appendices/con_guide _3.1.03.pdf.

Snow, C. E., Burns, M. S., & Griffin, P. (1998). *Preventing reading difficulties in young children.* Washington, DC: National Academy Press.

Spires, H. A., Gallini, J., & Riggsbee, J. (1992). Effects of schema-based and text structure-based cues on expository prose comprehension in fourth graders. *Journal of Experimental Education, 60,* 307–320.

Stanovich, K. E. (1986). Matthew effects in reading: Some consequences of individual differences in the acquisition of literacy. *Reading Research Quarterly, 21,* 360–407.

Stanovich, K. E. (1994). Romance and reality. *The Reading Teacher, 47,* 280–291.

Stahl, S. A. (1999). *Vocabulary development.* Cambridge, MA: Brookline Books.

Stahl. S. A., Richek, M. G., & Vandevier, R. (1991). Learning word meanings through listening: A sixth-grade replication. In J. Zutell & S. McCormick (Eds.), *Learning factors/teacher factors: Issues in literacy research.* Chicago: National Reading Conference.

Taylor, B., Pearson, D., Clark, K., & Walpole, S. (1999, September 30). *Beating the odds in teaching all children to read* (Ciera Report no 2-006). Ann Arbor: University of Michigan, Center for the Improvement of Early Reading Achievement.

Tharp, R. G. (1982). The effective instruction of comprehension: Results and description of the Kamehameha Early Education Program. *Reading Research Quarterly, 17,* 503–527.

Torgesen, J. K., & Mathes, P. (1998). What every teacher should know about phonological awareness. In *CORE reading research anthology.* Novato, CA: Arena Press.

Yatvin, J., Weaver, C., & Garan, E. (2003). Reading first: Cautions and recommendations. *Language Arts, 81,* 28–33.

Yopp, H. K., & Yopp, R. H. (2000). Supporting phonemic awareness development in the classroom. *The Reading Teacher, 54,* 130–143.

chapter four

What Are All These Assessments?

The new school year arrives with an explosion of activity. Sarah, in her second year of teaching, feels as though she's being challenged from all sides. New attendance protocols have been designed, not enough textbooks have arrived on time, and the copy machine is already out of order, but twenty-two grinning first graders are anxiously waiting at her door. Her resolve? They will all be reading at first-grade level or higher by the end of this year. Of course, she notes, some will have to learn English first. Hmm . . . and some will have to learn to sit in one place for more than thirty seconds too, she observes as one little boy bounces from one foot to the next in line.

Ellen is working as quickly as she can to get to know each of her students individually. Being with young children is why she chose this profession and the reason she stays. She understands that getting to know her students is the single most important thing she can do in the first few weeks of school. Then she will be better able to build on their needs and interests as the year progresses.

Both Sarah and Ellen are anxious to evaluate what their students know and are able to do in reading and writing so they won't waste any of their students' initial back-to-school enthusiasm. Knowing where to begin and what activities and books will engage their students are important first steps in beginning and growing a successful learning community.

The use of assessments to support instructional decisions and to drive school reform is not a new concept. Horace Mann challenged school officials to compare student scores on written exams in math, grammar, history, and geography and then he published the assessment results in his *Common School Journal* on October 1, 1845. Nineteenth-century Americans often viewed educational assessments as a form of community entertainment with spelling bees, ciphering contests, and oral recitations being a part of community activities and celebrations as well as a means of measuring student progress and providing an incentive to master lessons (Cremin, 1980).

The science of educational testing is almost 100 years old. During its advent, in the beginning quarter of the twentieth century, *The English Journal* described the phenomenon: "The science of measurements is in its infancy and its significance is still only vaguely understood by the profession and not understood at all by the public" (National Council of Teachers of English, 1917, p. 67). Almost ninety years later, much of the science of testing is even now only vaguely understood by teachers and school administrators, and the public is generally still as much in the dark as ever about the whys and hows of student testing.

Assessments and testing have today become a commonly anticipated and integral part of both teachers' and students' educational lives. They are regularly used in complying with state and district mandates and they provide information to design and organize instruction.

Although few educators have argued that testing is not a useful device for determining achievement levels for student performance and for preparation and lesson planning, some of us have worried that an overemphasis on testing may actually detract from classroom instruction time. Reading First schools have a large proportion of their resources delegated to assessing individual and collective student performance, and the results are intended to provide important indicators for early intervention for those students who are most at risk for reading difficulty. Through systematic, ongoing instructional assessments, individual children will be properly identified and assisted so they will perform at an expected level of achievement.

Reading First Assessment Plans

Each Reading First state has designed an assessment system to provide regular screening, diagnosis, progress monitoring, and outcome achievement information for its Reading First program. Although some states specified the actual assessment products, others left the choice up to districts, providing them with criteria to assure validity and reliability.

Valid and reliable assessment instruments must be used in specific core areas of reading instruction based on a regular and systematic master schedule to monitor progress and assist in instructional decisions. Initial steps include plans for purchasing assessment materials and training for the administration and data collection of the assessments. Dissemination of test results in combination with professional development activities help teachers identify students at risk for reading difficulties so they may be provided with extra or alternative instruction. Assessment results are reported by state, district, and site levels, and are disaggregated to determine progress of students by income, major racial groups, limited English proficiency, and special education populations.

Reading First Assessment Targets

A basic premise of Reading First is that assessments can provide information on reading outcomes that will influence informed instruction and essential intervention prior to third grade. For kindergarten, first-, and second-grade students, the purpose of the assessment is to identify difficulties early so additional instructional intervention can be provided to ensure grade level reading achievement outcomes by third grade. The core areas for instruction and assessment reporting include:

- Phonemic awareness
- Phonics
- Fluency
- Vocabulary
- Comprehension

Teachers must not only know the strategies and techniques for increasing student achievement in each of the essential components of reading instruction, but must also know how to assess student progress in each. Although assessment of phonemic awareness and phonics skills becomes less important in later grades, vocabulary and comprehension are life-long criteria against which literacy is measured. Spelling and writing, though not explicitly mentioned in the key elements, are essential tools to informed literacy instruction and are especially integral to phonics, vocabulary, and comprehension instruction. Training is sometimes necessary to administer, score, and interpret test results and in some cases is provided by the companies associated with testing products. Regularly scheduled meetings for teachers to evaluate and discuss classroom assessments and adjust instructional strategies are an integral part of Reading First goals and plans.

Types of Reading First Assessments

Screening—Who needs intervention instruction?

Screening assessments are administered to predict which students are at risk for reading difficulty and in need of additional diagnosis or intervention. The levels of required intervention can also be assessed. Some may require more concentrated attention, whereas others may need less intense but equally important assistance. A fundamental concern for screening assessments is predictive validity; that is, how well the results of the test can be used to predict future performance. Determining which students are most likely to experience reading difficulty is a first step in providing additional, appropriate instructional strategies to ensure student success in grade-level reading outcomes.

Screening assessments, as part of the total assessment system, must be closely aligned with outcome-based assessments so that effective early screening will target the correct student population for diagnostic and instructional planning.

Diagnostic Assessments—What Specific Areas of Instructional Intervention Are Needed?

Diagnostic assessments are administered to help teachers plan instruction by providing in-depth information about students' specific skill levels and instructional needs. Diagnostic assessments pinpoint which specific skill areas are sufficient and which need additional instructional intervention. Understanding which explicit skills require substantial additional instruction allows teachers to analyze which strategies may be systematically applied. Some interventions might include:

- Different instructional programs
- Smaller group instruction
- Different student groupings based on similar instructional needs
- Extra time
- More practice
- More modeling
- More scaffolding

Diagnostic assessments, including a variety of teacher-made or specialized assessments, should be an extension of screening assessments to provide practical related information. For example, once a student has been screened for difficulty with phonemic awareness, a diagnostic assessment can determine if that difficulty is a result of not mastering initial, ending, or medial sounds or perhaps a lack of skill at blending sounds. Like screening assessments, diagnostic tests must be aligned with outcome monitoring assessments to provide consistent support to struggling learners.

Progress Monitoring—How Well Are Interventions Working?

Progress monitoring assessments are administered at a minimum of three times a year to verify if students are making adequate incremental progress or if they need more or different interventions to achieve grade-level reading outcomes. All intervention plans cannot be guaranteed to work for all students. Because students have different levels of background knowledge and ways of coming to understand literacy and learning, not all interventions work equally well with all children. Progress monitoring assessments can provide ongoing, formative evaluation information. They identify rates of reading improvement, recognize students who are not demonstrating adequate progress, and provide evaluation of different forms of instruction. Accordingly, instruction may be modified on an individual basis if necessary, so that all students can achieve proficiency outcomes at the end of an instructional cycle.

Progress monitoring assessments should be synchronized with diagnostic interventions to help in understanding the effectiveness of instructional efforts on student learning. A routine of monthly or quarterly assessments, using comparable and multiple test forms will provide estimated rates of reading improvement and assist in identifying those students who are not demonstrating adequate progress. These students may then be offered additional or different forms of instruction.

A review of all screening, diagnostic, and progress monitoring information will provide a total profile of individual student progress and intervention attempts as well as their apparent successes and needs for improvement.

Outcome-Based Assessments—How Well Is the Entire Program Working?

Outcome assessments are administered as an evaluation of the effectiveness of the reading program. To comply with state accountability assessment requirements, students either meet grade-level expectations or show progression at a rate that indicates they will meet expectations in the state progress-monitoring accountability system. Screening and diagnostic assessments, as well as progress monitoring assessments, should be aligned with outcome-based assessments to provide a totally integrated evaluation system. States gather this data annually in terms of whether progress is being made in increasing the number of students who are reading at grade level or above and if the number of students who are reading below grade level has correspondingly been reduced. In addition, states report the increased percentages of students in certain special populations (i.e., ethnic, low-income status populations who are reading at grade level or above). Using a nationally norm-referenced assessment measure

- Students performing at least at the 40th percentile are likely to meet state accountability standards.

• Students performing between the 20th and 39th percentile will need additional instructional intervention to meet state accountability standards.

• Students scoring below the 20th percentile will need substantial instructional intervention to meet state accountability standards. (Paige, 2002)

Scientific Basis for Reading Assessments

Mastery of each of the essential components must be based on valid and reliable assessments. Assessments should be chosen on the basis of their scientific validity and reliability to provide accurate and useful information to assist instruction. Together, validity and reliability are used to establish the accuracy of measures and for determining how they should be used.

Validity

Validity is the degree to which a test measures what it is intended to measure and the inferences that can be made from measured results. Note the word "degree" in the definition. A test is not simply "valid" or "not valid." Because validity concerns the extent to which test results are useful in making decisions about instruction, there are varying degrees of validity. Validation is a process of gathering evidence to support accurate inferences that may be made from test score data. It is not the test itself that is validated, but the inferences regarding specific uses of the test. In order to provide appropriate, meaningful, and useful information, the test must be adequately aligned to the content that is being taught and measured. In standards-based assessments, this means that the instruction and the assessments are based on the goals and subject matter of the content standards established by each state.

Three types of validity evidence are commonly referred to:

1. *Construct-related validity.* From test results, inferences are made about the degree to which a student possesses some reasoning ability. Construct-related validity asks what test scores really mean in terms of a student's conceptual understanding.

2. *Content-related validity.* The sample of items in a test should be a fair and representative sample of the content and skills to be measured. Evidence of content-related validity is usually obtained by having knowledgeable experts look at the test items and make judgments about the appropriateness of each item and overall coverage of the standard being measured. Content-related validity asks if the test items are appropriately measuring the targeted content.

3. *Criterion-related validity.* Sometimes test results are used to make inferences about how a person might perform on a different domain. Criterion-related evidence may be used to predict a student's current or future test performance by correlating it with an existing and accepted measure. Criterion-related validity asks how accurately current or future criterion performance can be predicted from scores on the test.

To be valid, the purpose for the test must be well defined and each of the test items should be targeting a specific concept and skill level. By allowing for precision in purposeful test items, information can be better utilized to assist teachers with instructional decisions. You might think about it this way: When you are shopping and you weigh a bag of oranges or apples or any other fruit, you want to know the weight so you can determine the price. The color, texture, or taste of the fruit is not important at that moment. Likewise, if you are measuring phonemic awareness, the data you collect and analyze should be focused on the child's awareness of phonemes. You cannot expect that test to provide you with valuable information about a child's vocabulary or comprehension. For that, you will need a different test.

Who is responsible for determining test validity? According to *The Standards for Educational and Psychological Testing* amended in 1999 by the American Educational Research Association, the American Psychological Association and the National Council on Measurements in Evaluations state that, "Test users are responsible for evaluating the quality of the validity evidence provided and its relevance to the local situation" (www.apa.org/ppo/issues/phtestandx.html). Educators and others who use the test data to make educational decisions are in the best position to become familiar with the information provided by tests to make the final determination regarding whether the test is appropriate for the task.

Reliability

Reliability is the estimated degree to which test information accurately and consistently corresponds to what a test is attempting to measure. It is the extent to which scores obtained on a measure are reproducible in repeated administrations under the same conditions with the same or consistently comparable populations.

There are four general classes of reliability estimates, each of which estimates reliability in a different way.

1. *Test-retest reliability.* This technique is used to assess the consistency of a measure from one time to another by administering a test, then administering it a second time to the same or a similar set of test-takers after an interval of time.

2. *Parallel-forms reliability.* This method is used to assess the consistency of the results of two tests constructed in the same way from the same content with the same levels of difficulty.

3. *Internal consistency reliability.* Internal consistency measures are used to assess the consistency of results across items within a test. A wide variety of statistical measures may be used to evaluate internal consistency.

4. *Inter-rater reliability.* When open response items are scored, there is a varying amount of inconsistency between the scores given by different raters. Inter-rater reliability is used to assess the degree to which different raters or observers give consistent estimates of the same score on an assessment item.

Measurement error, or the level to which a measurement instrument indicates varying results from one administration to another, exists in all measurements, whether it be a weight watcher's bathroom scale or a consumer survey for the potential of a new product. Differences in equipment, situations, or participants' attitudes can all contribute to some degree to the precise reliability of measurement results. Test takers may, on different days, be more motivated or tired, or simply guess correctly more times. Because of this, student scores will typically not be perfectly consistent between two interchangeable forms of a test.

To be reliable, a test produces consistent test scores over different test administrations, with multiple raters, and for different test questions. Reliability asks how likely it is that a student would obtain the same results after repeated test administrations. Reliability measures are generally expressed as a decimal, with a level of .90 or higher considered extremely high.

Who is responsible for determining test reliability? Test developers are responsible for obtaining and reporting evidence concerning reliability and measurement errors to assist educators in using assessments as interpretations for student learning. Test users are responsible for determining that the information regarding reliability and measurement error is relevant to their intended uses and interpretations of scores. This responsibility on the end-user is similar to consumer responsibility in the commercial market place. For example, when you purchase a commercial cold medicine product that has been approved by the FDA and you are asked whether it works, imagine the reasons why you would never respond, "Since the drug has been approved by the federal government, I don't need to know whether it works for me or not." For the same reasons, we as responsible educators should always check the reliability and validity with our own students to assure the assessments being used to measure student proficiency are providing accurate and useful information to assist instruction.

Assessment of Key Elements

The importance of early evaluation of all the key elements is vital to accurately monitoring student achievement in Reading First schools. The National Institute for Literacy commissioned an analysis of reading assessment instruments to assist states and districts in selecting appropriate assessments to monitor K–3 student progress and achievement. It was designed

1. To create a process, criteria, decision rules, guidelines, rationale, and protocol for identifying and evaluating the selection of reading assessment instruments

2. To identify a set of scientifically valid, research-based assessment instruments with sufficient evidence for use as screening, diagnosis, progress monitoring, or outcome measures to assess one or more of the five essential elements defined in the Reading First legislation.

After reviewing twenty-nine popular measurement tools, the assessment committee found that twenty four of them had sufficient evidence for use as screening, diagnosis, progress monitoring, or outcome measures to assess one or more of the five essential elements in reading for one or more grades K–3. Information is available at the website: http://idea.uoregon.edu/assessment/index.html.

Assessments in Phonemic Awareness

The assessment of phonemic awareness (the awareness of sounds that make up spoken words) can include three categories: sound comparison (sound identity), phoneme segmentation, and phoneme blending.

Sound Comparison

Assessments to measure a student's phonemic awareness deal with students' oral recognition of

• Phoneme identity—recognizing the same sounds in different words (e.g., What sound is the same in ball and boot?)

• Phoneme isolation—recognizing individual sounds in a word (e.g., What is the first sound in bat?)

• Phoneme categorization—recognizing a word that doesn't belong in a series of related word sounds (e.g., Which word doesn't belong in the following set? Rug, ran, rope, bed)

Phoneme Segmentation

Another means of assessing student knowledge of phonemes is to ask them to segment a word into its discrete sounds such as picking out the number of sounds in the word "dog" or "spot."

• Phoneme segmentation—Breaking a word into its sounds by tapping out or counting the sounds by pronouncing and positioning a marker for each sound

• Phoneme deletion—Recognizing what word or word part changes when a sound is removed from or added to another word (e.g., What word is left if you take away the s in scat? Or, what word is made when you add an s to cat?)

Phoneme Blending and Manipulation

Students' abilities to verbally blend sounds aloud are other indicators of proficiency. An example might be to ask students, "What word has the /k/ /a/ /t/ sounds blended together?"

• Phoneme blending—combining separately spoken sounds into a recognizable word

• Phoneme manipulation—manipulating beginning, middle, and ending sounds within single-syllable words

Standardized assessments will sometimes provide students with a picture and ask them to choose from a variety of letters to select the correct beginning, ending, or medial sound of the word the picture represents.

Assessments in Phonics

Phonics, the sound–symbol relationships used to derive pronunciations of words, is usually assessed at the individual level because the application of phonics skills requires students to demonstrate their understanding of sounds and the symbols that represent them. Students are asked to demonstrate their knowledge of

- The alphabet
- Letter sounds and phoneme–grapheme correspondences
- The concept of word in text
- Word recognition in isolation
- Word recognition in context

Phonics assessments consist of several subtests that are designed to measure student knowledge of beginning, middle, and ending sounds; digraphs; blends; vowels; and words in isolation. Exercises are provided where students create, add, delete, or change sounds to make word patterns and rhyming words. Subtests may include assessments on initial single consonants, consonant blends, consonant digraphs, short vowel sounds, long vowel sounds, vowel digraphs, reversals, inflectional suffixes, derivational suffixes, prefixes, and compound words.

Spelling subtests may consist of a developmental spelling inventory—a list of words organized in increasing levels of difficulty. This helps obtain information about students' knowledge on a variety of spelling features or patterns. A spelling inventory provides a means of examining a student's developmental knowledge of letter–sound relationships, and facilitates planning for word study instruction.

Assessments in Fluency

Students must read with sufficient fluency to enable them to focus on the meaning of a text rather than merely identifying the written words. Fluency and oral reading skills are measured for accuracy, automaticity, and prosody. In classroom-based assessments, students are usually asked to read orally and respond to a short passage they have already read silently. An analysis is made of their oral reading fluency by looking for evidence of their use of phonics, sight vocabulary, semantics (concepts of word meanings), and syntax (sentence structures).

Accuracy

Accuracy is measured by the percentage of words read aloud correctly. These percentages are used to estimate a student's reading level. According to conventional readability estimates, students reading with 99 percent accurate word recognition and at least 90 percent comprehension are reading at an independent level; those reading at 95 to 98 percent accuracy and comprehending at 75 to 89 percent are reading at an instructional level; and those reading at less than 90 percent accuracy and comprehending at lower than 50 percent are attempting to read text that is at a frustration level. Figure 4.1 provides a rubric for determining reading levels.

FIGURE 4.1   Criteria Rubric for Reading Levels

Independent Level Reading

Independent reading level is the highest level at which a child can read the material without assistance.

- The reader demonstrates 99 percent accuracy in word recognition. Reading is fluent and rhythmical. There are few, if any, deviations from print and those that do occur do not affect meaning.
- Responses to comprehension items or retellings are completed with 90 percent or greater accuracy. Reader's reactions reflect a thorough understanding of material. Retellings are organized and replicate the organization of the passage.

Instructional Level Reading

Instructional level is the highest level at which a child will benefit from teacher directed instructional support.

- The reader demonstrates 95 to 98 percent accuracy in word recognition. (Note: With teacher support, that can be as low as 90 percent.) Oral reading is fluent, but at times is more mechanical than smooth. Although a few deviations from print may affect meaning, most are self-corrected.
- Answers to comprehension items or retellings demonstrate good understanding with approximately 75 to 94 percent accuracy. Retellings reflect organization of the passage with no serious intrusions or distortions. Although minor misinterpretations may occur, the reader is able to manipulate and critically respond to ideas presented in the passage.

Frustration Level Reading

Frustration level is the lowest level at which a child is likely to be frustrated, even with instructional support.

- Errors in word recognition occur for more than 90 percent of the text. Reading is slow, labored, and nonfluent. Deviations from the text affect meaning and oral rereading does not afford improvement over initial reading.
- Reactions to questions or retelling are at less than 75 percent accurate and reveal a lack of understanding about organization of passage, poor recall of details, and/or misinterpretation of passage content. Reactions to prereading discussions may suggest lack of language or background experience for understanding the selection.

Adapted from Johnson & Pikulski (1987) and McKenna & Stahl (2003).

Automaticity

Automaticity is the fluent processing of information that requires little effort or attention. It is generally assessed using a words-per-minute rate of oral reading in instructional-level text.

Grade 1   80 words per minute
Grade 2   90 words per minute
Grade 3   110 words per minute

Sight words, that is all words that a student determines on sight or automatically, should be recognized at the approximate rates given above.

Prosody

According to *The Literacy Dictionary,* prosody is "the pitch, loudness, tempo, and rhythm patterns of spoken language" associated with oral reading (Harris & Hodges, 1995, p. 196). Students use knowledge of basic conventions (e.g., punctuation and capitalization) to read aloud smoothly and easily in familiar text. Efforts to evaluate prosody analyze students' abilities to read in larger, meaningful phrase groups rather than word by word. Although repetitions, self-corrections, regressions, and some text errors may occur, the overall reading of a fluent reader maintains the sentence structure as presented in the text and is done with expressive interpretation.

The National Center for Education Statistics, sponsored by the U.S. Department of Education, has developed a rubric to assist in evaluating student prosody. As show in Table 4.1, it provides four levels of descriptive benchmarks.

DIBELS

Many Reading First sites have adopted *The Dynamic Indicators of Basic Early Literacy Skills* (DIBELS) as an assessment tool for reading fluency. The DIBELS measures were developed at the University of Oregon with assistance from a federal grant. The use of these materials is free and they can be downloaded at http://dibels.uoregon.edu/dibels. DIBELS includes a set of standardized, individually administered measures of early literacy development. They are one minute fluency measures used to monitor the development of prereading and early reading skills in phonological awareness, alphabetic principles, and fluency as measured by word counts per minute.

Assessments in Vocabulary

Vocabulary, an essential component of proficient reading, speaking, listening, and writing, is the ability to understand and use words to acquire and convey meaning. Vocabulary tests consisting of assessments of word knowledge—active or passive, oral or silent—are perhaps the best predictors of student comprehension

TABLE 4.1 Oral Reading Fluency Scale

Level 1	Reads primarily word by word.	Occasional two-word or three-word phrases may occur, but these are infrequent.
Level 2	Reads primarily in two-word phrases with some three- or four-word groupings.	Some word-by-word reading may be present. Word groupings may seem awkward and unrelated to larger context of sentence or passage.
Level 3	Reads primarily in three- or four-word phrase groups.	Some smaller groupings may be present. However, the majority of phrasing seems appropriate and preserves the syntax of the author. Little or no expressive interpretation is present.
Level 4	Reads primarily in larger, meaningful phrase groups.	Although some regressions, repetitions, and deviations from text may be present, these do not appear to detract from the overall structure of the story. Preservation of the author's syntax is consistent. Some or most of the story is read with expressive interpretation.

Source: Adapted from the National Center for Education Statistics, http://nces.ed.gov/pubs95/web/95762.asp.

(McKenna & Stahl, 2003). Without knowing the meanings of most of the words they have decoded, students will not be able to understand what they have read. Both listening and reading vocabulary should be assessed in the earliest stages of literacy learning.

Teachers can assess a student's vocabulary as part of fluency or comprehension tests by asking the student for meanings of difficult words. Unknown words may be recorded on recording forms such as running records. In vocabulary assessments, students are asked to do some or all of the following:

- Select meaning by word or select word by meaning.
- Classify and sort groups of words into categories.
- Discern which word from a group of words does or does not belong.
- Use visual and contextual clues to read and understand words and sentences.
- Choose the correct word meaning (sometimes as a synonym or antonym) from a list of multiple choices.
- Decode and demonstrate understanding of root words, base words, affixes (prefixes and suffixes), compound words, contractions, and inflectional forms.

- Determine the correctly or incorrectly used homophone (same sound, different meaning) or homograph (same spelling, different meaning).
- Complete a sentence or phrase from a selection of words with only one being a reasonably correct response.
- Display ability to apply dictionary skills.
- Demonstrate understanding of thematic vocabulary.

Table 4.2 provides vocabulary assessment examples.

Assessments in Comprehension

According to the National Reading Panel (2000), comprehension strategies are conscious plans or procedures that good readers use to help their awareness of how well they are comprehending as they read and write. Comprehension measurements of narrative, descriptive, expository, and persuasive texts examine the processes that readers use to make meaning of content and to communicate their understanding of what was read.

Both listening and reading comprehension are usually measured using a question-and-answer process that can provide for a range of difficulties and types of understanding (Pressley & Afflerbach, 1995). In a testing situation the student either listens to or reads a passage and is then asked to do one or more of the following in a multiple-choice or constructed-response format:

- Predict elements of the passage using text features and previous understanding to make logical and informed predictions about the continuation of the reading. (Example: Based on what you just read about the character, what do you think he/she will do next? Why?)

- Locate specific information and details. (Examples: Find where the text says . . . ; describe the setting or characters; identify main idea as it is clearly stated in the text.)

- Retell the passage, including as many important details as the student can recall in a sequential reconstruction of the text. (Example: What happened first, next, how did the story end?)

- Summarize important parts of the text by condensing larger parts into smaller pieces. (Example: Using just a sentence or two, tell what just happened on that page.)

- Make inferences or generalizations derived from information and observation. (Examples: Identify how the character or setting contributes to the story; describe characters based on actions in the text; make general statements from informational details; determine the author's purpose.)

- Analyze text and form judgments based on the text and reasonable conclusions. (Examples: Identify implied main idea or moral of a story; evaluate reasons or alternative solutions to a problem.)

- Evaluate the ability of the text to achieve its purpose. (Examples: effective use of details for support, likelihood of event taking place, adequacy of explanation)

TABLE 4.2   Vocabulary Assessment Examples

Assessment	Example
Select meaning by word or select word by meaning. A word or definition of a word is provided orally or in writing and must be matched.	A *swill* is a a. furry creature b. type of flower c. food for pigs d. brisk wind (answer: a food for pigs) Another name for an animal that is awake at night and sleeps during the day is a. sleepy b. nocturnal c. noxious d. serene (answer: nocturnal)
Classify/sort groups of words into categories. Students group given words by meaning or concept.	Sort the following words: train, car, sun, boat, rain, clouds, plane, snow, and shuttle. 1. Weather: sun, rain, clouds, snow 2. Transportation: train, car, boat, plane, shuttle
Discern which word from a group of words does or does not belong.	Given the following words, pick the one that does NOT belong: book, magazine, fruit bar, map (A fruit bar cannot be read.)
Use visual and contextual clues to read and understand words and sentences.	As I carefully climbed up the steep mountain, I was careful not to *stumble* over rocks. What does the word *stumble* mean?
Choose the correct word meaning (sometimes as a synonym or antonym) from a list of multiple choices, flash cards, or bingo game cards.	Circle the correct choice in each. 1. Which means the same as *meager*? low, slow, poor, thick 2. Which is the opposite of *fast*? race, hope, stop, slow
Decode and demonstrate understanding of root words, base words, affixes (prefixes and suffixes), compound words, contractions, and inflectional forms.	If preread means to read before, what does prearrange mean?

TABLE 4.2   (continued)

Assessment	Example
Determine the correctly/incorrectly used homophone (same sound, different meaning), or homograph (same spelling, different meaning).	1. Draw pictures to show the differences in meaning between the words *meet* and *meat*. 2. Choose the correct choice for the two meanings of dove below. The *dove* flew up into the tree as Becky *dove* into the water. a. bug–leaped b. bird–jumped c. kite–flew d. wind–blew
Complete a sentence or phrase from a selection of words with only one being a reasonably correct response.	Only a very *imprudent* person would ride a bike without a helmet on a busy highway. Choose the word below that means the same thing as *imprudent,* as used in the sentence. a. foolish b. popular c. happy d. important
Display ability to apply dictionary skills.	Using your dictionary find at least two meanings for the word *bank.*
Demonstrate understanding of thematic vocabulary.	Circle all the words below that have to do with frogs. reptile, nest, webbed, tadpole, pond, wing, mammal, eggs, fish, bugs, croak, cubs

In cloze tests, students are sometimes assessed by being asked to identify words that have been systematically eliminated from a given text. Students must choose the answer that correctly completes the blank in the passage. At other times students are required to read a passage or view a picture and choose from a selection of words to best complete a phrase or sentence. For example, after viewing a picture of a park on a clear day, the test item might be

The day in the picture is
a. rainy
b. sunny
c. cloudy
d. snowy

Classroom-Based Assessments

Classroom-based assessments are generally derived from teacher observations, student interviews or discussions, or individually or group-administered tests. They typically are based on individual student performance, and progress is compared to previous individual levels of performance or to grade-level expectation as empirically determined by test developers.

Oral and Written Assessment Connections

Systematic observations of children's daily learning, often done in an informal manner, are used to evaluate and establish instruction in reading and writing. Anecdotal notes, records of teacher–student conferences, and collections of student performance data provide teachers and students with measurements of growth and targeted items for additional student effort and teacher instruction. Ongoing evaluation, based on interpretation of children's reading behaviors, oral skills, and writing activities play an important part of daily literacy instruction.

Informal Reading Inventories

Informal reading inventories (Johnson, Kress, & Pilkuski, 1987) vary in the amount of reading achievement data collected. Some are more comprehensive than others and may include oral decoding and silent reading as well as listening comprehension measurements. An informal reading inventory is an individually administered reading test that consists of a series of graded word lists followed by leveled passages and a comprehension test. The student is provided with a reading passage and the test administrator has a duplicated copy on which to note miscues and student responses. As the student orally reads a passage, the test administrator records any reading miscues (e.g., omissions, insertions, hesitations, substitutions, mispronunciations) and some general observations on the fluency of the reading. Then, the student is asked a series of comprehension questions to determine his or her level of understanding. This too is recorded by the administrator.

The student may then silently read several progressively more difficult passages, sometimes under timed conditions, with additional comprehension questions. Once the student is reading passages at frustration level (less than 90 percent word recognition and more than 50 percent comprehension errors) the test is concluded. After the number of words read per minute and the levels of correct comprehension questions are recorded, the results are analyzed to determine a student's independent, instructional, and frustration levels of text. These results help to determine appropriate grouping and materials for instruction so the child is successful and also somewhat challenged. (See Figure 4.1 for reading levels.)

Miscue Analysis

Analysis of student miscues in a passage can provide insight into student misconceptions and cueing strategies they use in reading text. The teacher provides the student with a passage to read aloud independently. The oral reading can be taped for later analysis. The teacher listens to the tape and uses a chart to record the text wording in one column and what the student has actually read in the next column. All miscues, including substitution, omissions, insertions, mispronunciations, reversals, and successful and unsuccessful corrections, are included. Percentages are calculated based on the total number of miscues; the miscues and miscue patterns are then analyzed based on graphic similarities and differences, syntax, semantics, and self-correction attempts. By doing a miscue analysis, an appraisal of a student's need for additional instruction to improve reading can be based on the kinds of reading strategies he or she uses or ignores.

Running Records

Running records, developed by Clay (2000), record student reading behaviors quickly and easily in a relatively informal setting. They can be used with any appropriate text based on a student's instructional level (i.e., at least 90 percent accurate word recognition). Like miscue analysis, running records provide an indication of the cueing systems that a student knows how to use and which strategies may need further instruction. The coding system for correctly pronounced words is a check mark above the correct word. Miscues that involve substitutions or insertions are written by the teacher, omissions are recorded by placing a dash mark above the omission area, and self-corrections and variations of teacher assistance are indicated by initialed coding. After the student reads the story he or she must retell it and may return to the text for clarification or may receive occasional teacher prompting if needed.

Later the teacher determines the accuracy rate, error rate, and self-correction rate and analyzes the source of the miscues: meaning (M), structure (S), or visual (V) cues. Meaning cues are those that indicate the student may have used sentence context or perhaps picture cues to determine if the word made sense. Structure cues involve syntax, and are generally noted in students who reread a passage to determine what "sounds correct" based on recognizable grammatical formats. Finally, visual cues, also called *graphophonics systems,* are apparent when students analyze a word phonetically or attempt to decode it based on similar looking or sounding words.

Running records assist in monitoring ongoing student progress and determining which particular skills and strategies students are using (i.e., meaning, structure, or visual) to provide balanced instruction. Although some teacher rehearsal and practice in using this system may be necessary for proficient and rapid administration, having this kind of information about students is valuable in grouping students for instruction and in determining specific lessons to introduce or reinforce.

Norm Reference and Criterion Reference Tests

A test comparing a student's performance to a norm or average of performances by other, similar students is called a norm reference test. Norm reference test results allow policy makers, the public, and educators to look at increasing and decreasing trends in student achievement across different populations and localities to determine where to best provide resources and assistance to help all children reach their literacy potential.

Criterion reference tests, rather than comparing students' scores to one another, provide information on a student's skill level according to established criteria. School, district, and state results are provided as percentages of students mastering specific skills or objectives.

Making Sense of Norm Reference or Criterion Reference Test Score Reports

As educators we often serve as interpreters in helping parents and the general public understand achievement performances based on norm reference test reports. Because of this, we need to be prepared with information on assessment terms and their relative importance in determining instructional goals and plans.

Types of Statistical Scores

- *Raw scores*—Show the number of items answered correctly on a test.

- *Composite scores*—The arithmetic average of subtest scores in one or more areas.

- *Scaled scores*—Statistically converted scores used to weigh items differentially, with designated rates of proficiency levels.

- *Standard scores*—Scores that indicate relative position within a particular distribution of scores; a number that represents any score quantity (e.g., percentile rank, percent, raw score) in terms of standard deviations, or a fraction of a standard deviation, in a normal distribution (e.g., a *z* score).

- *Percentile rank*—Compares students' scores with one another in a ranked order. Students scoring in the 40th percentile are considered on grade level. Students scoring between the 20th and 40th percentile need additional intervention. Students scoring below the 20th percentile need substantial intervention.

- *Quartiles*—Commit individual scores into a one-quarter norm group; categorize the score into one of four sections.

- *Stanine*— Indicates a student's relative standing in a reference group. Represents the raw scores in a band of one to nine, with the fifth position being the 20 percent in the middle. The most accurate way to interpret stanine scores is to determine the band around the score (e.g., a 64th percentile is more accurately understood as being between the 58th and the 88th percentile).

- *Developmental benchmarks*—A predetermined goal or score defined as meeting expectations of proficiency for each developmental level. It remains stable so that outcomes can be compared from year to year.

- *Normal curve equivalent*—Commits individual scores into ninety-nine statistically equivalent sections.

- *Grade-equivalent score*—Estimates of the grade level corresponding to a given student's raw score. Generally used to compare an individual student's performance with a normative sample. (Sprinthall, 2003)

Assessing Student Motivation and Engagement in Reading

Reading First goals are not only directed toward the abilities to read and write, but also toward students' positive attitudes about literacy processes. Although some of today's students know how to read, they choose not to. This issue is as difficult to deal with as is illiteracy in the classroom.

Teachers must assess students not merely on their levels of reading ability, but also on their interests in reading and their attitudes toward literacy events as a means of informing instructional activities. McKenna and Stahl (2003) suggest classroom observations, anecdotal records, analysis of student reading logs, and the administration of surveys, questionnaires, and interest inventories to gather information on appropriate materials and lessons for instruction. In addition, McKenna and Stahl include an elementary reading survey that may be photocopied for classroom use. Reutzel and Cooter (2003), besides recommending attitude surveys, also propose the use of socially constructed literacy events to engage students in the meaningful literacy interactions (e.g., book clubs, literature circles, grand conversations, and other student-centered reading approaches). (For a thorough listing and explanation of engaging literacy activities see also Tompkins, 2004). They also advise the use of reader response strategies in authentic and motivating ways by providing students with the means of developing creative products (e.g., dramatic representations, visual art products, or written responses based on reading).

Teachers may want to use the following guide and suggestions in observing, assessing, and evaluating their students' reading motivation.

1. *Purpose.* Does the student seem to understand that the purpose of reading is to understand and make meaning of text?

Reading aloud to students provides those without decoding skills the ability to participate in a literacy community in which ideas are discussed and the benefits of reading are demonstrated.

2. *Student reading stamina.* To what extent does the length of the passage or the time spent reading influence a student's ability to stay focused?

Gradually increasing reading time over an extended period will provide students who have short attention spans with the ability to stay focused for longer and longer periods of time.

3. *Background knowledge and vocabulary.* Does the student seem to possess the necessary background knowledge and vocabulary to understand self-selected texts?

Prereading discussions and vocabulary surveys prior to reading will assist these students. Electronic texts with hyperlinks are helpful for students who don't have the necessary background vocabulary for a text.

4. *Genre preference.* Does the student demonstrate different reading rates and amounts of text consumed when reading fiction versus informational text?

Discuss the varying rates and styles of reading, depending on the purpose for reading any text. Allow sufficient time with varying genres to accommodate differential reading rates.

5. *Self-correction strategies.* To what extent does the student demonstrate self-monitoring and correction strategies with difficult text?

Having the skills and strategies to tackle difficult text makes for confident readers who are not easily discouraged. Establishing a risk-free learning environment that recognizes varying levels of development in all learning areas will be perhaps the best motivation for struggling readers to continue to strive for success.

According to a position statement by the American Association of School Librarians (www.ala.org/ala/aasl/aaslproftools/positionstatements/aaslpositionstatementvalueindependent.htm), and the International Reading Association (www.reading.org), to become life-long readers, students must have

- Access to current, quality, high interest, and extensive collections of books and other print materials, including material from the Internet

- Contact with adults, especially parents and teachers, who read regularly and widely and who serve as positive reading role models

- Time during the school day and at home, during which students can read for pleasure, information, and exploration

- Opportunities that involve caregivers, parents, and other family members in reading

Reading Assessment Information Websites

Analysis of Reading Assessment Instruments for K–3: http://idea.uoregon.edu/assessment

> The Institute for the Development of Educational Achievement (IDEA) in the College of Education at the University of Oregon provides a list of assessments specifically addressing Reading First components.

Reading Assessment Database for Grades K–2: www.sedl.org/reading/rad/welcome.html

> The Southwest Educational Development Laboratory provides a searchable database that describes in detail readily available early reading assessment tools.

Focus on Reading Assessment: www.reading.org/focus/assessment.html

> The International Reading Association provides position statements, publications, and information on meetings and events related to reading assessment issues.

Assessment in Higher Education: http://ahe.cqu.edu.au/index.htm

> The University of Queensland, Australia, website contains information on assessment terminology.

The Early Literacy Network: http://literacy.edreform.net

> Part of the Education Reform Network (http://edreform.net), the Early Literacy Network is a catalog of resources promoting early literacy.

References

American Educational Research Association, American Psychological Association, and National Council on Measurement in Education. (1999). *Standards for educational and psychological testing.* Washington, DC: American Educational Research Association. Retrieved December 20, 2003, from http://www.apa.org/ppo/issues/phtestandx.html.

Clay, M. M. (2000). *Running records for classroom teachers.* Portsmouth, NH: Heinemann.

Cremin, L. A. (1980). *American education, the national experience, 1783–1876.* New York: Harper & Row.

Harris, R. L., & Hodges, R. E. (Eds.). (1995). *The literacy dictionary: The vocabulary of reading and writing.* Newark, DE: International Reading Association.

Johnson, M. S., Kress, R. A., & Pikulski, J. J. (1987). *Informal reading inventories* (2nd ed.). Newark, DE: International Reading Association.

McKenna, M. C., & Stahl, S. A. (2003). *Assessment for reading instruction.* New York: Guilford.

National Council of Teachers of English (NCTE). (1917). *Proceedings of the sixth annual meeting, New York City, November 30 and December 1–2, 1916. English Journal, 6*(1), 40–68.

National Reading Panel (NRP). (2000). *Teaching children to read: An evidence-based assessment of the scientific research literature on reading and its implications for reading instruction.* Washington, DC: National Institute of Child Health and Human Development.

Paige, R. (2002). Lead and manage my school: Key policy letters signed by the Education Secretary or Deputy Secretary. Washington, DC: U.S. Department of Education. (Available online at www.ed.gov/policy/elsec/guid/secletter/020724.html.)

Pressley, M., & Afflerbach, P. (1995). *Verbal protocols of reading: The nature of constructively responsive reading.* Hillsdale, NJ: Erlbaum.

Reutzel, D. R., & Cooter, R. B., Jr. (2003). *Strategies for reading assessment and instruction.* Upper Saddle River, NJ: Merrill/Prentice Hall.

Sprinthall, R. C. (2003). *Basic statistical analysis* (7th ed.). New York: Pearson.

Tompkins, G. E. (2004). *Fifty literacy strategies: Step by step* (2nd ed.). Upper Saddle River, NJ: Pearson/Prentice Hall.

U.S. Department of Education, National Center for Education Statistics. (1995). *Listening to children read aloud.* Washington, DC: Author. Retrieved July 3, 2004, from http://nces.ed.gov/pubs95/web/95762.asp.

chapter five

The Implications and Issues Surrounding Reading First Legislation

On the Friday before spring break, Ellen is straining to hold the attention of her third graders. Sarah, across the hall, is doing likewise with her first graders. Dedicated teachers like Ellen and Sarah will continue to persevere, inspiring us daily with their efforts and professionalism as they work at making readers out of nonreaders. There are some teachers who manage to reach students beyond all obstacles.

Reading First legislation has some teachers, principals, and state departments of education personnel worried about whether they can meet the expectations of this legislation. They ponder questions such as: What happens if my school or classroom is not using scientifically based strategies and materials? What happens if children in my school do not do well on all of the assessments that are required, and do not demonstrate growth in reading? What happens if my state does not have evidence that more children are reading at grade level or above by third grade? These questions are important to ponder and they are certainly serious and carry heavy penalties if not achieved. This is the part of the legislation that has many states, districts, and schools frustrated and angry.

Instead of centering their concerns and energy on these possible sanctions, teachers are focusing on students. We want educators to seriously consider the current body of research centered on reading and writing and bring the best recommendations from this research to the everyday practices of teachers in classrooms. Our guiding question is: What action can teachers, schools, districts, and state departments take to best utilize the financial and professional resources of Reading First legislation to meet the needs of individual students and support them in their quest for literacy knowledge and understanding?

In answering this question, we organized this chapter around the implications and issues surrounding Reading First legislation. We considered the larger context of reading reforms, reports, and books that have influenced reading education and then moved to a consideration of the classroom and how this specific legislation will change or modify practices within it by considering potential consequences of this legislation.

Reading Reforms

Although teachers may see policy as something distant, something that does not touch their teaching or the learning of their students, the reality is that policy does touch the lives of students, teachers, principals, and district and state educational leaders on a daily basis. Historically, there have been many federal policy documents, reports, and books that have affected the learning experiences and teaching practices of classrooms in America.

Federal Policies

Federal educational policies are typically developed through a synthesis of the recommendations of educational research, expert testimony from practitioners, data from schools (such as achievement data), and compelling individual cases. Although these disparate sources drive policy decisions, recently there has been more reliance on educational research as seen in the Reading Excellence Act and Reading First legislation. Both of these federal acts have required teachers to use scientifically based research to support the literacy teaching practices they employ.

One of the first major federal influences on education was the 1965 Elementary and Secondary Education Act. This act resulted in Title I and Head Start Programs, among other initiatives. More current are the policies that were developed under the presidencies of Bill Clinton and George W. Bush.

During Clinton's administration there was the America Reads Initiative that supported volunteers to help children learn to read at grade level by the end of third grade. In 1997, there was also the legislation of the Reading Excellence Act. This act had four major goals:

1. Teach all children to read in the primary grades.
2. Improve the reading skills of students by having teachers use practices that are supported through reliable, replicable research.
3. Expand the number of high-quality family literacy programs.
4. Reduce the number of children referred to special education. (http://www.ed.gov/offices/OESE/REA/index.html)

When this legislation was enacted, it allocated about 327 million dollars to a number of states to support the improvement of reading skills and the use of scientifically based reading instruction. Approximately forty states received this support. The primary activities were professional development, tutoring, family literacy, and transition programs for kindergartners.

The most current federal policy directed toward education is the No Child Left Behind (NCLB) legislation which is a major revision of the Elementary and Secondary Education Act (National Institute of Child Health and Human Development, 2000). Shannon (2000) reported that this legislation was enacted to correct the perceived failures of the Reading Excellence Act. Among the perceived failures was insufficient monitoring of schools and student achievement and their use of scientifically based reading instruction and materials.

Although Shannon (2000) sees the NCLB legislation as positive for it is focused on scientifically based reading programs, not all literacy experts agree. Allington and Nowak (2004) believe that Reading First looks to "commercial curriculum packages (proven programs) as the way to improve reading instruction" (p. 99). They continue by criticizing policymakers in believing that a program will change the achievement of children in low performing schools.

Others like the Fordham Foundation (Brady, 2003) are also not convinced that NCLB will make a significant difference to student achievement. Brady writes that although NCLB contains very prescriptive mandates, "little is known about what kinds of interventions are most likely to turn faltering schools into successful educational institutions" (p. iii).

The goals of Reading First legislation, in particular, have been identified in detail earlier in this book. However, Reading First is different from previous legislation through several of its expectations and requirements. Some of these are:

1. *Adequate yearly progress (AYP).* All children in schools must demonstrate adequate yearly progress to retain federal money. Schools must report this data in a

disaggregated format in which they identify groups of children within each school (e.g., the achievement of Hispanic students, black students, special education students, and so on).

If a school does not meet AYP expectations, there are sanctions for the failing school, district, and state. In schools that do not meet AYP, parents can place their child or children in other schools and a portion of the school's federal funds may then be reallocated for this purpose. If a school does not meet AYP for four years, they are subject to state takeover. States can also lose Reading First dollars if Reading First schools do not show achievement gains for primary-grade students.

This is one of the most challenging requirements of Reading First and NCLB. Recently, adjustments have been made to these expectations for ELL students. Currently, some states and districts are petitioning the federal government to lesson these expectations.

2. *Scientific methods and materials.* Schools and teachers are expected to only use methods and materials that have research support. In Reading First schools, for example, all programs and materials must be evaluated as to their scientific base.

This is difficult to do because few independent researchers have evaluated an entire program. Often publishers conduct their own studies but these are viewed with skepticism because it is hard for a company to be unbiased when they conduct research on a product they are marketing. Later in this chapter there will be discussion as to how to critically evaluate a core reading program.

This expectation has also received criticism. Allington and Nowak (2004) suggest that policymakers must understand that there is no single program that can reach the needs of all students. Darling-Hammond (1997) similarly cautions against a one-size-fits-all approach to teaching reading. Although these concerns are valid and there are serious questions about the scientific basis for an entire program, Reading First policymakers never mandated that the materials or programs be used exactly the same with all students. In fact, they expect schools and teachers to provide interventions for struggling readers and writers.

3. *Ninety-minute uninterrupted literacy block.* Teachers are expected to provide a daily, ninety-minute block that is totally focused on reading instruction.

As teachers, we believe this is one of the most valuable expectations of Reading First. Teachers can offer students time to read in thoughtful ways and to provide necessary direct instruction to groups of students or individuals. Most schools have added to this literacy block, however. They have found that there is not sufficient time to teach all of the language arts within this time. In addition, they have another hour block for writing instruction, a half-hour block for direct instruction in writing, and a final half-hour block for instruction targeted to intervention for children who are struggling or to advanced instruction for gifted and talented students.

Reports

One of the earliest reports to impact instruction in schools was the First Grade Studies (Bond & Dykstra, 1967/1997) organized by the U.S. Office of Education in the 1960s. The study was organized to answer the following three major questions:

1. To what extent are various pupil, teacher, class, school, and community characteristics related to pupil achievement in first-grade reading and spelling?
2. Which of the many approaches to initial reading instruction produces superior reading and spelling achievement at the end of first grade?
3. Is any program uniquely effective or ineffective for pupils with high or low readiness for reading?

Although the questions were conceived in the 1960s, they still are current issues as researchers continue to seek answers to them, particularly the one concerning effective programs. To answer the above questions, the researchers organized twenty-seven individual projects throughout the United States. These studies found that phonics instruction and letter knowledge were predictive of future reading achievement. However, the most frequently cited result of this study is that the quality of the teacher was the most important variable to student achievement.

In the 1980s there were two major reports that influenced education. The first report was *A Nation at Risk* (National Commission on Excellence in Education, 1984). This report documented the situations in schools and identified education as necessary for the security of our nation. It highlighted how U.S. preeminence in commerce, industry, science, and technology was being overtaken by other countries. They determined that it was mediocre education that caused this situation and that schools should return to having higher expectations for student learning (www.ed.gov/pubs/NatAtRisk/risk.html). The report did not focus solely on reading; rather, it highlighted how all curriculum should become more rigorous for students so that the United States would regain its preeminence in the world.

The second report, *Becoming a Nation of Readers* (http://my.execpc.com/~presswis/nation.html), was specific to reading instruction in classrooms and in homes. This report defined reading in broader terms than had been considered before. The definition included the ideas that skilled reading is constructive, skilled reading is fluent, skilled reading is strategic, skilled reading is motivated, and skilled reading is a lifelong pursuit. In addition to this definition, the authors of the report highlighted the importance of parents in helping children learn to read, the importance of phonics instruction, and that reading instruction should be focused on meaning. Shortly after this report was published, teachers began bringing children's literature into their classrooms and moving away from more basal-centered instruction.

In 1998, the National Research Council published the report, *Preventing Reading Difficulties in Young Children* (Snow, Burns, & Griffin, 1998). Similar to *Becoming a Nation of Readers,* this report suggested ways to teach young children to read. The report again emphasized the importance of gaining meaning from reading. In addition, it supported providing extensive time for children to engage in reading; instruction in phonics, particularly regular spelling-sound patterns; teaching the alphabetic writing system; and helping children understand the structure of spoken words.

Congress was unhappy that this report did not specify how critical reading skills should be taught (Edmonson, 2004). They then convened a panel (the National Reading Panel) to explore reading research to determine which strategies proved effective in teaching young children to read. The National Reading Panel's report served as the foundation for Reading First legislation.

Classrooms and schools have certainly been changed instructionally, as can be seen through this brief overview of federal legislation and reports. In the 60s classrooms focused on phonics and letter knowledge, and in the 80s classrooms included more children's literature and a greater focus on meaning. In the late 90s and early 2000s, the focus on reading and writing maintained a meaning orientation; however, a greater emphasis on phonemic awareness, phonics, comprehension, fluency, and vocabulary are evident.

The power of the reports and legislation can be easily seen in publisher's materials and current books written for teachers of literacy. For example, as we scanned the most current *Reading Teacher,* we found numerous advertisements detailing how commercial programs support Reading First legislation or the key components of reading instruction (e.g., phonemic awareness, phonics, fluency) and are scientifically based. Moreover, organizations like the International Reading Association have grouped recent books together that support teachers and schools in meeting the Reading First mandate of having K–3 children become successful readers. These books are seen as a source of material to stimulate professional conversations around literacy and students.

The International Reading Association (IRA) has also published a statement dealing with the U.S. government and its policies concerning reading (www.reading.org/positions/reading_policy.html). In this position statement, the organization supports the federal government's interest in literacy and in making it a priority in the national education agenda. The IRA sees Reading First as an "opportunity to address the critical needs classroom teachers confront on a daily basis" (IRA, 2001, n.p.). They also report on the responsibilities of this organization, which include participating in dialogue with those who draft and implement this policy and in sharing this dialogue with IRA members. Additionally, the IRA will provide consultation to policy drafters, advocate for the best interests of schools and children, and will make every effort to have reading professionals as a part of the process. This policy statement is one of the many produced by IRA and can be found on their website (www.reading.org).

Books

Why Johnny Can't Read and What You Can Do About It (Flesch, 1955) was one of the first books to hit the best-sellers list that was addressed to parents on how they could help their child learn to read. Flesch blamed schools for using the whole-word method and not teaching children to read. He saw reading failure as a national epidemic and phonics as the single solution to this catastrophe. In addition to providing the background to this situation, he provided material that parents could use to help their child read better.

In 1967, Jeanne Chall wrote the book *Learning to Read: The Great Debate.* Her book also criticized the whole-word method of teaching reading that was popularized through Dick and Jane basal readers. Chall built a case for synthetic phonics and the explicit teaching of phonics skills to young children. This book was one of the first to state that explicit, synthetic phonics instruction provided an advantage for high poverty youngsters in learning to read.

In 1971, Frank Smith wrote *Understanding Reading.* Unlike Chall's and Flesch's books, this book focused on meaning and how children come to understand text. Rather than focusing on decoding individual words, Smith argued that children could predict words from the meaning of the text and their background knowledge. His writing led the way to major changes in classroom instruction that deemphasized explicit phonics instruction and focused on meaning. Later these practices came under attack as part of what was commonly called whole language instruction.

In 1990, Adams wrote her book, *Beginning to Read.* In her book, she summarized the research base and how it supported beginning reading instruction. Her book made strong connections between what was known in the research base and how it translated into instruction. Not surprisingly, her book strongly emphasized the need for phonics instruction with young readers. She also highlighted phonemic awareness knowledge as essential for reading development.

There are certainly numerous other books that have had an impact on early literacy. We have selected just a few for you to consider. The work of Smith and the work of Adams, among others, triggered what have been called the *Reading Wars.* These wars were centered on whole language and skills-based instruction, and which one should be used to the exclusion of the other. In the 2000s, most educational researchers argue for balance, meaning that literacy instruction for young children should include both skills- and meaning-based instruction. (For an additional exploration of the importance of policies, reports, and books to early reading instruction see Pressley, Allington, Wharton-McDonald, Block, & Morrow, 2001).

From the Big Picture to Reading First

Potential Negative Consequences

Limited research may be considered. Reading First and its foundational report, the National Reading Panel report, are grounded in a limited research base. Due in part to time constraints, the National Reading Panel report narrowed the work it included to a limited number of quantitative studies. Although these studies are important to understanding effective literacy practices, they do not include all of the careful research that has been conducted relative to student achievement in literacy. The NRP report provided much in the way of answering *what* questions, but it did not provide practitioners with sufficient information on the *why* questions that are such an integral part of qualitative studies. For example, Pressley, Dolexal, Roehrig, and Hilden (2002) criticized the NRP report for not including research on early language development and its connections to later reading achievement.

Others, like Allington (2002), have also written about the problems they see with the National Reading Panel report.

The NRP report has its strengths and its problems, and we worry that teachers and schools will rely only on what is written in this report to guide instruction. If this happens, classrooms will be limited to a small subset of the research and, perhaps worse, they will be excluded from any research that has occurred since the report was written.

For example, Teale (2003) posed questions that teachers should ask and that research studies should consider. Some of these questions include:

• What does typical literacy development look like across the early childhood years?

• What patterns of development characterize children's transition from emergent to conventional literacy?

• What roles do factors like a young child's sociocultural and linguistic background, as well as his or her motivation to learn, play in the literacy learning process?

• What kinds of classroom oral language activities contribute significantly to early literacy learning?

• How much do independent reading activities help children become capable, comprehending readers?

• Which types of texts help beginning readers learn to read?

These are just a subset of the significant questions he offers that do not have clear answers in our current research. Some of the questions may seem surprising and even disappointing in that there are no definitive answers in the research. Teachers might expect that there is existing research documenting which texts best support young readers, but this work has yet to be conducted or reported on.

If researchers follow Teale's charge, there will be significant new research that answers important questions for teachers. In addition, Teale (2003) considered questions directly related to policy decisions like those in Reading First. He writes, "Community-based, state-level, and federal policies help early literacy research findings, curriculum materials, instructional techniques, family literacy programs, and other effective practices to be implemented in home, child care, preschool, school, and teacher education settings" (p. 36). To build from his statement, there are incredible research opportunities centered around legislation like Reading First. A few possible questions might be:

• How do teachers and schools bring research-based practices into their classrooms on a systematic basis?

• How effective is the professional development surrounding Reading First legislation, and how does it affect different groups of teachers and teachers who serve different populations of students?

- What research-based practices are most easily implemented in classrooms after professional development?

- Which practices are the most difficult to implement?

- What research-based practices best support the literacy learning of English language learners?

As you can see, it is not difficult to generate important questions centered on this legislation. These questions require partnerships among researchers, teachers, and students, as well as support from policy-making bodies.

Because Reading First is based on research in the National Reading Panel report, it is important for teachers to be familiar with all of the details of the report—and we mean the whole report, not the summary document. (The summary document is not consistent with the results of the whole report.) However, even though this report is extensive, it does not share all of the knowledge necessary for teachers as they make instructional decisions related to reading and writing. Therefore, it is very important for teachers to consider other research not included in the report, such as qualitative research, and research not targeted by the report, such as research surrounding the learning and instruction for ELLs. It is critically important for teachers to stay current with the latest research by routinely reading journals, books, and websites that share this information, and then sharing this information with colleagues and administrators.

This expectation is not an easy one to achieve. It is time consuming and often frustrating, because clear answers to simple questions are not always evident or available. As we suggested earlier in this chapter, keeping up with current research about literacy instruction is best done within communities of educators. Through sharing the research, teachers are able to discern the strengths and problems of implementing new strategies, for example.

Teachers may feel controlled and limited in how they teach.   We worry that teachers may see Reading First legislation as controlling and limiting as to their choices of instruction or curricular materials. These beliefs may restrict the materials or instructional strategies they use and result in the choice of scripted reading programs. Jennings (1996) worries that the federal scientifically based program mandate will result in scripted teaching manuals and a single classroom–based lesson schedule. Similarly, we believe that such rigid programs treat all students as though they are the same, in that the same instructional sequence is deemed appropriate for all students.

Although teachers and administrators may interpret the Reading First legislation in this way, we do not believe this has to be the case. Reading First asks teachers and schools to identify students who are struggling with reading development. These children are to receive additional literacy instruction beyond the ninety-minute uninterrupted block to ensure their literacy success. Most importantly, Reading First highlights the importance of assessment driven instruction. This implies that teachers are expected to teach to the unique strengths and needs of individual students.

Teachers, with the support of literacy specialists, are to carefully consider the instruction and learning of a child through progress monitoring assessment and then determine what the best literacy intervention might be to accelerate the learning of this child. Each child is treated as an individual with intervention tied directly to his or her strengths or needs. This interpretation carefully matches the child with additional instruction to support his or her literacy development.

This type of instructional sequence requires teachers to be especially cognizant of the strengths and needs of their students through ongoing informal assessments and more formal progress monitoring assessments. Following from the use of these assessments, is an expectation that teachers have a wide repertoire of research-based practices and materials to support students as they develop into more competent readers and writers. As Neuman and Roskos (1998) wrote, "Because children's development varies, so too must our instructional strategies. It is imperative for teachers to be familiar with a wide variety of explicit teaching approaches, materials, and strategies to enrich children's understanding of literacy" (pp. 7–8).

Rather than limiting teachers, this act expects more from them. It expects that

- Teachers understand how to assess students and then how to match instruction based on this assessment.

- Teachers know when students need additional support beyond the typical instruction provided in their classroom.

- Teachers understand the current scientific research centered on literacy and how to implement its findings in the classroom.

- Teachers understand how to evaluate the materials they use to determine their scientific soundness.

These expectations are extensive, and require new levels of expertise for teachers—levels of knowledge and understanding that were not expected in the past.

No emphasis on the instruction for gifted and talented students.   Reading First targets low achieving students and expects that teachers and schools will bring them all to grade level achievement. The worry then becomes what will happen to grade level and above grade level achieving students?

In some schools this focus on low achieving students could seriously limit the opportunities for gifted and talented students. This would be true if teachers relied only on one textbook with a fixed schedule of delivery. Caution is warranted here, for in Reading First schools teachers are expected to have fidelity to their chosen reading programs and directly teach all students in the same way for the ninety-minute literacy block.

If teachers provide the same curriculum for all students, gifted students could become bored and develop behavior problems. Their instruction would not match their achievement potential and learning would not be accelerated. The intent of the legislation was surely not to close the achievement gap by lowering the student levels of achievement. Teachers will need to find time and the means to extend the grade level curriculum so that these students come away with an expansion of their current knowledge and understanding about reading and writing. All students should be given the opportunity to reach their maximum potential for intellectual growth.

Schools and districts might only focus on potential sanctions.   Critics state that the sanctions associated with the No Child Left Behind act are punitive and will not help schools and districts provide the necessary instructional support for students. Neill (2003) believes that "Education will be seriously damaged, especially in schools with large shares of low-income and minority children" (p. 225). He suggests that in schools in which students do not perform well, "there will be pressure to eliminate or reduce emphasis on such untested subjects as history, science, language, and the arts" (p. 225). Further, he believes that a majority of schools will not meet the adequate yearly progress provision of the NCLB act; and because of this, schools will need to use a portion of their Title funds for tutoring or to support the transfer of students to other schools. His final criticism is the federal government has not provided significant funds to implement all of the provisions of NCLB legislation.

Neill's view is important to consider because the learning expectations for Reading First are enormous. Teachers and administrators could narrowly focus on only these issues and the difficulties surrounding them. They can worry that the students in their school will not demonstrate literacy achievement and they will be punished. They can be pessimistic and wait for the dismal results of their students, and the resulting punitive consequences.

Or teachers can understand the potential sanctions and become proactive about helping students learn to read and write more effectively and efficiently than they have done in the past. Teachers might begin with an exploration of what the literacy instruction and materials are at their site. For example, how do first-grade teachers instruct children in reading and writing? What are the core reading materials? From this exploration, the teachers, staff, and principal might explore the National Reading Panel report together and determine if their practices match what is recommended in this report. If they do, they might want to explore other research that targets a portion of their student population that they feel needs more support. If their instruction doesn't match what is recommended in the report, they might consider how they will make changes to their instruction and what important instructional decisions they will make to change the instructional environment at their school. Figure 5.1 provides an assessment tool to evaluate the physical literacy environment at a school and Figure 5.2 provides an assessment of teachers' knowledge of the key literacy components. Teachers can use the results of these tools to guide the purchase of materials and ongoing professional development. For example, if the analysis shows that there are few nonfiction books in the school, then a priority would be to secure more. Or, if teachers only relied on comprehension questions following reading to teach comprehension, then professional development would be targeted to other comprehension strategies.

FIGURE 5.1   Assessing School Literacy Materials

	Yes	No
The School Library		
1. The school library has adequate informational and narrative text for all students in the school.	❏	❏
2. The school library has leveled text for students.	❏	❏
3. The school library has text that is related to the major units of study in social studies and science.	❏	❏
4. The school library has magazines that are of interest to students.	❏	❏
5. The school library has Internet access for students and teachers.	❏	❏
The Classroom		
1. The classroom has an adequate library with informational and narrative text that matches and exceeds the students' reading instructional reading levels.	❏	❏
2. The classroom has a core reading program and there is evidence of its systematic use.	❏	❏
3. The classroom has numerous leveled books available to students for independent and small group reading.	❏	❏
4. The classroom walls have support materials for students such as the alphabet, word wall, and word study explorations.	❏	❏
5. There is Internet access for the teacher and students.	❏	❏
6. There are supplies for writing and evidence that students routinely engage in writing.	❏	❏

Reading First expects that schools will use the current research base to guide instruction and that the materials students experience match this base. This expectation allows for much discussion and collaboration among teaching staffs to reflect on their current practices and determine if and what changes should be made to target the learning potentials of all students. We see this as an opportunity that takes the focus away from the sanctions connected with this legislation.

Potential Positive Consequences

Teachers and schools will apply scientifically based practices in their classrooms and student proficiency will show marked improvement.   Research since at least the First Grade Studies (Bond & Dykstra, 1967/1997) has consistently identified

FIGURE 5.2   Assessing Teachers' Knowledge about Literacy Elements

What is phonemic awareness?

List two or three ways you would teach phonemic awareness.

1.

2.

3.

What is phonics?

List two or three ways you would teach phonics.

1.

2.

3.

What is comprehension?

List two or three ways you would teach comprehension.

1.

2.

3.

FIGURE 5.2   (continued)

What is fluency?

List two or three ways you would teach fluency.

1.

2.

3.

What is vocabulary?

List two or three ways you would teach vocabulary.

1.

2.

3.

Directions: After teachers have completed the above assessment, identify any misconceptions that teachers have about the literacy elements. Following this clarification, identify the major strategies that teachers use for each element. Use this information to guide professional development activities.

how important the teacher is to the success of students. Following are a few quotes documenting this importance and how it is tied to beliefs and practice:

> Teachers' beliefs and expectations, particularly about individual differences between learners, have direct and indirect, positive and negative, influences on children's learning. (Johnston & Allington, 1991, p. 996)

> Good first teaching begins with a belief that all children can learn to read and write. (Fountas & Pinnell, 1999, p. 165)

> Qualified and talented teachers are essential if effective, evidence-based reading instruction is to occur. (Farstrup, 2002, p. 1)

> Every method can succeed with most children if taught well by a good teacher. That does not mean that some methods are not better or easier to teach well than others. (Cunningham & Creamer, 2003, p. 344)

> The best teachers weave a variety of teaching activities together in an infinitely complex and dynamic response to the flow of classroom life. . . . It is more like orchestration than straightforward implementation. (Duffy & Hoffman, 2002, p. 376)

These quotes highlight the complexity of exemplary teaching and its critical importance in the learning success of students. They also recognize that a teacher's beliefs about students influence instruction and the learning outcomes of those students.

Clearly, it is important that teachers are aware of the most current research that highlights practices that support the literacy learning of students. Simultaneously, it is important for teachers to take these findings and transform them into practices that target the learning needs of their students at their specific learning site.

Reading First receives one billion dollars per year, with its major goal being improvement of the reading achievement of children, especially those in high poverty, low achieving schools. This legislation provides for professional development for teachers through reading academies that target the current scientific base for reading instruction. Knowing that a single academy is not sufficient for professional development, Reading First schools have a literacy specialist/coach to support the day-to-day instructional change and decision-making processes of teachers.

Allington and Cunningham (2002) state that

> The only strategy we know for creating schools where all children become readers and writers involves creating schools where all teachers are more expert than most teachers are today. We need to create schools that make it easier for expert teachers to act on their expertise, but developing and refining the expertise of every teacher must become the primary focus of any elementary school hoping to become a good school—where all children become readers and writers. (p. 17)

We believe that Reading First, through its professional development expectations, provides opportunities for schools to engage in professional development centered on literacy research and to continue the dialogue about practice within school settings. Furthermore, the reading specialist/coach in Reading First schools can take leadership, along with the principal, to facilitate conversations centered on research and practice and how to target research that highlights the needs of students particular to their school.

Teachers will become leaders in consuming and creating research. There is no doubt that the charge of Reading First is for teachers to be careful consumers of literacy research. We have discussed this extensively throughout this book. Perhaps what is new is the role of teachers in creating research. Pressley (2002) discussed research methods used in reading education. He talked about experiments, correlational studies, and qualitative research. He ended his chapter by arguing that "School-based folks need to spend time studying that [scientific] edge as well, for they have a role in advancing the science, too" (p. 43). His message is an important one, for he found that by observing teachers and talking with them, he, and others, learned more about comprehension strategies than had been researched up until that point.

Stanovich and Stanovich (2003) concur that research conducted by teachers that considers their practice and student learning benefits the improvement of teaching practices in broader terms. These authors believe that systematic inquiry is a part of teaching, as seen in teachers' instructional decisions that are a result of informal assessment. They are suggesting that teachers move their systematic study from one that is personal and influences instructional decisions in their classrooms, to a more public one in which other teachers and researchers can use their results to extend the current body of research evidence, and thus provide converging evidence to educators.

Although we as teachers may be saying that this is too much to expect of us, there is increasing evidence of partnerships of researchers and teachers who have been able to design research studies that combine the best of theory and its connections to practice. Pressley (2002) states:

> Good educational scientists spend their time with good educators, just as good educators think about the cutting edge of educational science. As a result, good educational scientists and good educators become better educational scientists and educators together. (p. 43)

When teachers consider some of the current research, they may recognize how much of it has been accomplished through collaboration between teachers and researchers. A few examples are the work of Anne Dyson (1997) and her research with teachers to learn about young children's writing development, and the work of Michael Pressley and others (2001) in their exploration of what makes an exemplary first-grade teacher.

Teachers will become aware and participate in policy development.   Recently, teachers have organized and formed study groups in schools and they explore particular topics of interest and importance such as improving the comprehension or vocabulary skills of their students. Although we tend to think of these study groups as focusing on a literacy element or a specific age group of students (e.g., adolescents or early readers), there is no reason why teachers could not engage in policy discussions or in discussions that consider what others may think about public education.

Edmondson (2004) suggests that teachers visit sites such as the North Central Regional Educational Laboratory (www.ncrel.org) to learn about federal policies as a source for discussion. Although this site is extensive, there is one section devoted to NCLB. Within this section, there are resources that help teachers understand all of the requirements of NCLB and numerous articles about this act. She also recommends that teachers read the report *Where We Are Now: 12 Things*

You Need to Know About Public Opinion and Public Schools (www.publicagenda.org), written by Public Agenda. This report shares the results of numerous surveys of parents, teachers, students, principals, superintendents, and state boards of education from the years 1998 to 2000. This report highlights points of convergence and dissonance in ideas and opinions shared by the public and educators. Following are the key findings from this report:

1. The public, including parents, teachers, and students, believe that setting standards and enforcing them promotes learning. Social promotion harms kids.

2. Standards and promotion policies have changed in recent years, and attitudes about local schools have improved. Even so, many students still move ahead without acquiring needed skills.

3. The vast majority of parents and teachers say standardized tests are useful, and few students are overly anxious about them. But people also think tests can be misused, and many say there's too much emphasis on them.

4. Although teachers support higher academic standards, they have qualms about some aspects of testing.

5. Teachers are troubled by a lack of parental support and poor student behavior. Teachers also say their views are generally ignored by decision makers.

6. Americans say all students need the basics, and parents want their own children prepared for college. For many, a college diploma is as indispensable as a high school diploma used to be.

7. There is a dramatic gap between the way employers and college professors rate high school graduates and the way parents and teachers view them.

8. The vast majority of employers and professors continue to have serious doubts about public school graduates' basic skills, especially when it comes to writing.

9. Teachers say lack of parental involvement is a serious problem. According to both teachers and parents, parental involvement should focus on what goes on at home rather than on school management issues.

10. Teachers, parents, and students continue to voice concern about the rough-edged, uncivil atmospheres in many high schools. Few see high schools as places of respect or civility.

11. Superintendents and principals say their biggest problems are politics and bureaucracy. Most want more autonomy over their own schools.

12. Holding schools and educators directly accountable for student achievement is still uncommon. Teachers and principals have doubts about it, whereas parents and the public tend to support it.

In addition, teachers might read the *Kappan* or visit the Kappan website (www.pdkintl.org) in September to view the annual Phi Delta Kappan/Gallup Poll of the public's attitudes toward public schools, written by Alec Gallup and Lowell Rose. They might also review this poll over several years to note the differences in opinions about public schools over time.

Focused discussions on policy and public opinion help teachers understand a more global view of public education. Edmondson (2003) writes, "such a study is a crucial first step in our work toward recognizing what is valuable about certain policies as we simultaneously strive to bring policy changes" (p. 427). And certainly as teachers engage in these discussions, the result will be that they will become active in policy development related to education in the future.

Children will successfully develop as readers and writers.   Although some teachers, administrators, and the public may believe that there is a crisis in reading achievement that has never been experienced before, the data do not support this (Murphy, 2001). The overall reading achievement of students in the United States has remained stable since the 70s (Taylor, Hanson, Justice-Swanson, & Watts, 2000). What Murphy (2004) identified as the real issue is that there are changes in the criteria used to judge literacy. "Society is demanding higher reading levels than ever before" (Hall & Moats, 1999, p. 4).

In addition to higher expectations for what qualifies as reading proficiency, there are issues centered on the percentages of struggling readers in schools and those that represent certain groups of students (e.g., minority and high poverty students) who have continuously struggled with learning to read and write proficiently. Many studies indicate that about 20 percent of students find learning to read difficult (Foorman, Fletcher, Francis, & Schatschneider, 1998; Hall & Moats, 1999). If we believe that reading is an important skill that contributes to future success, then it is critical for educators to do better in fostering literacy achievement for all students. Not surprisingly, this is what Reading First asks of teachers.

Throughout this book we have discussed ways that teachers and schools can support students to enhance their literacy achievement. Chapter 3, in particular, provides a basis for teachers to use as they identify the research-supported practices that they currently use. Teachers are also encouraged to engage in collaborative conversations that focus on instructional strategies and on the children within their schools. A close look at students' performances will help teachers target instruction and interventions that will help children develop as readers, so that they can achieve reading and writing benchmarks by third grade, if not sooner.

Final Thoughts

Reading First can be considered an opportunity or an obstacle. Teachers' and schools' perspectives will be critical to the success or failure of this legislation. The goals of Reading First are hard to argue against: Increased student achievement in literacy, teachers who are aware and can implement scientifically based practices, and teachers and schools who use scientifically based reading programs and materials. The focus can be on these goals or it can be on the difficulties with this legislation, such as sanctions placed against schools that fail to demonstrate annual yearly progress for students. We believe that it is in the best interests of students, teachers, principals, researchers, and parents to provide exemplary, scientifically based reading and writing instruction to students with an end in sight—high levels of literacy achievement for *all* students.

References

Adams, M. (1990). *Beginning to read.* Cambridge, MA: Harvard University Press.

Allington, R. (2002). *Big brother and the national reading curriculum.* Portsmouth, NH: Heinemann.

Allington, R., & Cunningham, P. (2002). *Schools that work: Where all children read and write* (2nd ed.). Boston: Allyn and Bacon.

Allington, R., & Nowak, R. (2004). "Proven programs" and other unscientific ideas. In D. Lapp, C. Block, E. Cooper, J. Flood, N. Roser, & J. Tinajero (Eds.), *Teaching all the children: Strategies for developing literacy in urban settings* (pp. 93–102). New York: Guilford.

Bond, L., & Dykstra, R. (1967/1997). The cooperative research program in first-grade learning. *Reading Research Quarterly, 2* and *32,* 5–142.

Brady, R. (2003). *Can failing schools be fixed?* Washington, DC: Fordham Foundation.

Chall, J. (1967). *Learning to read: The great debate.* New York: McGraw-Hill.

Cunningham, J., & Creamer, K. (2003). Achieving best practices in literacy instruction. In L. Morrow, L. Gambrell, & M. Pressley (Eds.), *Best practices in literacy education* (2nd ed., pp. 333–346). New York: Guilford.

Darling-Hammond, L. (1997). *The right to learn: A blueprint for creating schools that work.* San Francisco: Jossey-Bass.

Duffy, G., & Hoffman, J. (2002). Beating the odds in literacy education: Not the "betting on" but the "bettering of" schools and teachers. In B. Taylor & P. D. Pearson (Eds.), *Teaching reading: Effective schools, accomplished teachers* (pp. 375–388). Mahwah, NJ: Erlbaum.

Dyson, A. (1997). *Writing superheroes: Contemporary childhood, popular culture, and classroom literacy.* New York: Teachers College Press.

Edmonson, J. (2004). Reading policies: Ideologies and strategies for political engagement. *The Reading Teacher, 57,* 418–429.

Farstrup, A. (2002). There is more to effective reading instruction than research. In A. Farstrup & J. Samuels (Eds.), *What research has to say about reading instruction* (pp. 1–7). Newark, DE: International Reading Association.

Flesch, R. (1955). *Why Johnny can't read and what you can do about it.* New York: Harper and Row.

Foorman, B., Fletcher, J., Francis, D., & Schatschneider, C. (1998). The role of instruction in learning to read: Preventing reading failure in at-risk children. *Journal of Educational Psychology, 90,* 255–276.

Fountas, I., & Pinnell, G. (1999). *Matching books to readers: Using leveled books in guided reading. K–3.* Portsmouth, NH: Heinemann.

Hall, S., & Moats, L. (1999). *Straight talk about reading: How parents can make a difference during the early years.* Chicago: Contemporary Books.

International Reading Association (IRA). (2001). *On U.S. government policy on the teaching of reading.* Newark, DE: Author.

Jennings, N. (1996). *Interpreting policy in real classrooms: Case studies of state reform and teacher practice.* New York: Teachers College Press.

Johnston, P., & Allington, R. (1991). Remediation. In R. Barr, M. Kamil, P. Mosenthal, & P. Pearson (Eds.), *Handbook of reading research* (Vol. II, pp. 984–1012). New York: Longman.

Murphy, J. (2001, October). *Leadership for literacy: Policy leverage points.* Princeton, NJ: Educational Testing Service.

Murphy, J. (2004). *Leadership for literacy: Research-based practice, pre k–3.* Thousand Oaks, CA: Corwin Press.

National Commission on Excellence in Education. (1984). *A nation at risk.* Washington, DC: Government Printing Office.

National Institute of Child Health and Human Development (NICHD). (2000). *The Report of the National Reading Panel. Teaching children to read: An evidence-based assessment of the scientific research literature on reading and its implications for reading instruction.* (NIH Publication No. 00-4769). Washington, DC: U.S. Government Printing Office. (Available online at www.nichd.nih.gov/publications/nrp/report.)

National Reading Panel (NRP). (2000). *Teaching children to read: An evidence-based assessment of the scientific research literature on reading and its implications for reading instruction.* Washington, DC: National Institute of Child Health and Human Development.

Neill, M. (2003). Leaving children behind: How No Child Left Behind will fail our children. *Phi Delta Kappan, 85,* 225–228.

Neuman, S., & Roskos, K. (1998). Introduction. In S. Neuman & K. Roskos (Eds.), *Children achieving: Best practices in early literacy* (pp. 1–19). Newark, DE: International Reading Association.

Pressley, M. (2002). What I have learned up until now about research methods in reading education. *National Reading Conference Yearbook, 51,* 33–44.

Pressley, M., Allington, R., Wharton-McDonald, R., Block, C., & Morrow, L. (2001). *Learning to read: Lessons from exemplary first-grade classrooms.* New York: Guilford.

Pressley, M., Dolexal, S., Roehrig, A., & Hilden, K. (2002). Why the National Reading Panel's recommendations are not enough. In R. Allington (Ed.), *Big brother and the national reading curriculum* (pp. 75–89). Portsmouth, NH: Heinemann.

Shannon, P. (2000). "What's my name?" Politics of literacy in the latter half of the 20th century in America. *Reading Research Quarterly, 35,* 90–107.

Smith, F. (1971). *Understanding reading.* Hillsdale, NJ: Erlbaum.

Snow, C., Burns, M., & Griffin, P. (1998). *Preventing reading difficulties in young children.* Washington, DC: National Academy Press.

Stanovich, P., & Stanovich, K. (2003). *Using research and reason in education.* Washington, DC: National Institute for Literacy.

Taylor, B., Hanson, B., Justice-Swanson, K., & Watts, S. (2000). Helping struggling readers: Linking small-group intervention with cross-age tutoring. In R. Robinson, M. McKenna, & J. Wedman (Eds.), *Issues and trends in literacy education* (2nd ed., pp. 267–283). Boston: Allyn and Bacon.

Teale, W. (2003). Questions about early literacy learning and teaching that need asking—and some that don't. In D. Barone & L. Morrow (Eds.), *Literacy and young children* (pp. 23–44). New York: Guilford.

index